Living in Morocco

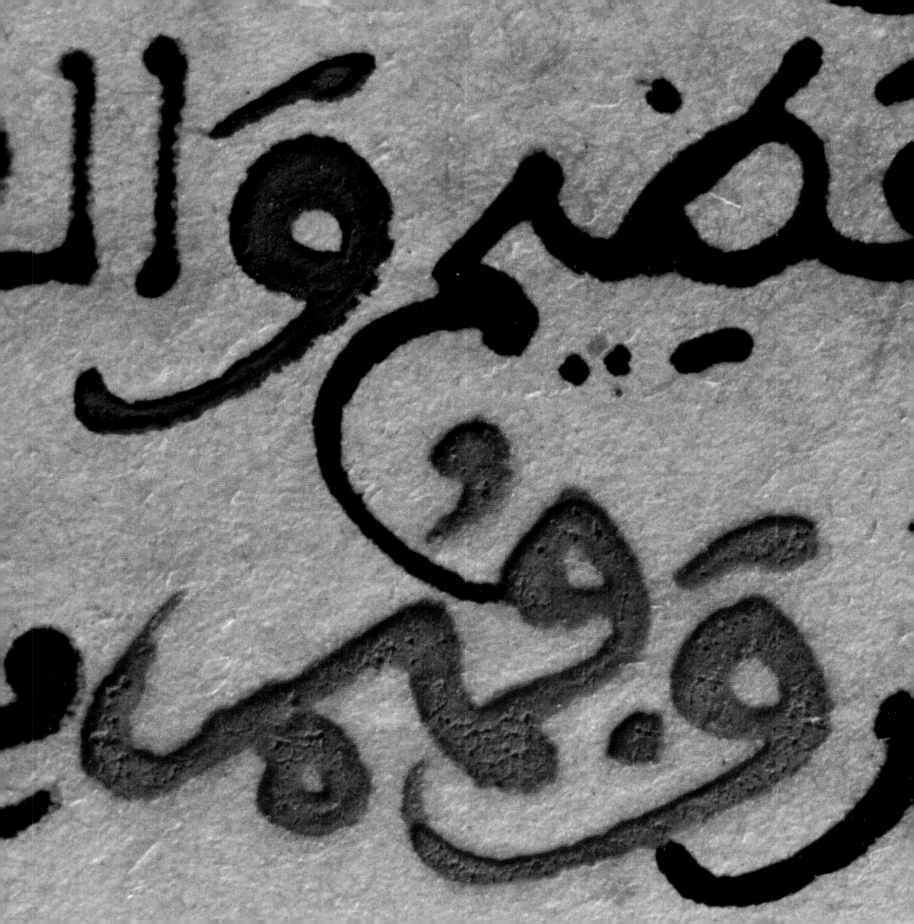

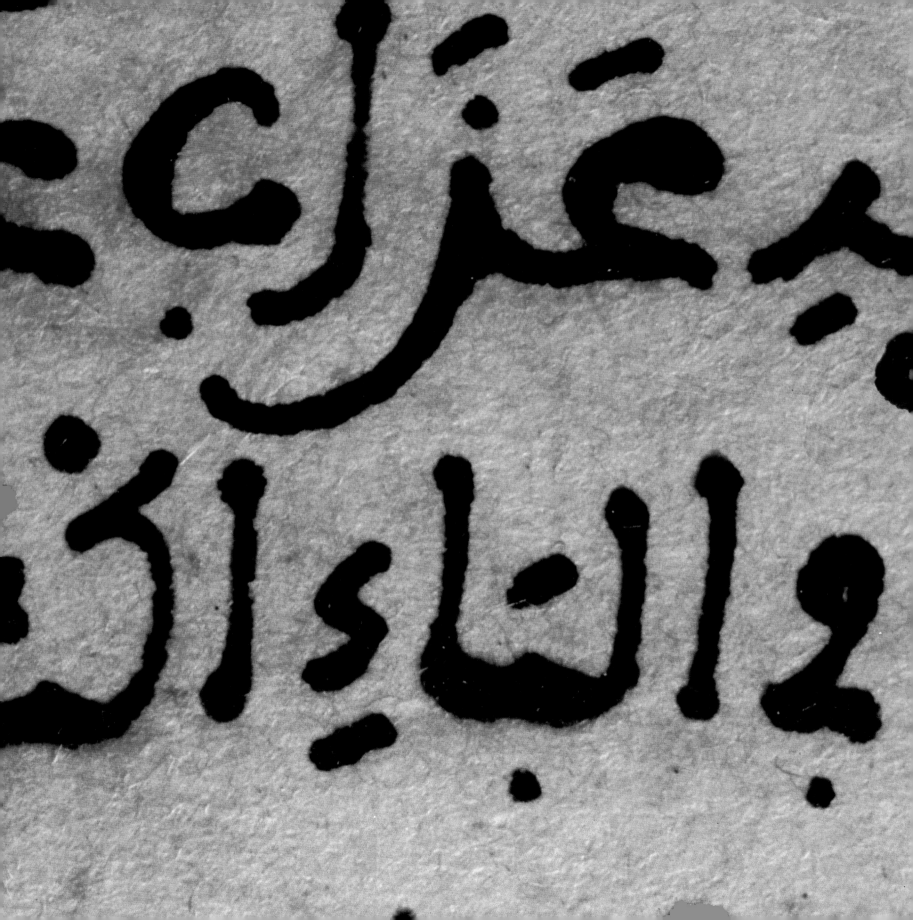

With 346 colour photographs

Photographs by Lisl Dennis
Text by Landt Dennis

Living in Morocco

Design from Casablanca to Marrakesh

Thames & Hudson

PAGES 2—3:
In spring, kasbahs and ksour—
such as these in the Dades Valley
on the edge of the
Sahara—are surrounded by
orchards in bloom.

PAGES 4—5:
Crenellated walls
wrap around Asilah,
a fishing village and artists'
colony on the Atlantic
coast near Tangier.

PAGES 6—7:
The detail of a 17th-century
illuminated manuscript
in Arabic is from the collection
of noted scholar
Mohamed Sijelmassi.

PAGES 8—9:
A palm stands in
stark contrast to the soft red
walls of Essaouira.

PAGES 10—11:
Whitewash covers the
walls of the tomb of a *marabout*,
or holy man, in Safi.

First published in the United Kingdom in 1992
by Thames & Hudson Ltd, 181A High Holborn,
London WC1V 7QX

www.thamesandhudson.com

© 1992 and 2001 Lisl and Landt Dennis

This revised edition published in paperback in 2001
Reprinted 2007

British Library Cataloguing-in-Publication Data
A catalogue record for this book is available from
the British Library

ISBN 978-0-500-28264-9

Printed and bound in China by
Toppan Printing Co Ltd

Tunisia is a woman, Algeria is a man, Morocco is a lion.
Arab saying

The first thing one should own is a home; and it is the last thing one should sell, for a home is one's tomb this side of heaven.
Moroccan proverb

When things come from the heart, the world is very small.
Hassan II

Contents

Introduction

THE FILM *CASABLANCA* AND ITS CAST—INGRID BERGMAN, HUMPHREY Bogart, Claude Rains, and Sydney Greenstreet—are legendary. But what of Morocco? ✋ A Muslim country with a population of 24 million—65 percent are Arab, 35 percent Berber—Morocco is a constitutional monarchy roughly the size of California. It is separated from Europe by the Strait of Gibraltar, bordered by the Atlantic to the west and the Mediterranean to the north. Algeria is to the east, Mauritania and the Sahara Desert are to the south. The Rif Mountains hug the Mediterranean coast; the Anti Atlas, High Atlas, and Middle Atlas Mountains form the country's spine. In fact, 70 percent of Morocco is mountainous. ✋ The country has an almost unequaled climate. Days of sun and temperatures that range from the forties to the nineties Fahrenheit allow for a wide range of flora and fauna—from oaks, pines, and palms to cork, cedar, eucalyptus, and citrus trees. In the spring, before the summer heat, wild flowers grow in profusion along the coastal plains and in the valleys. Orange and yellow marigolds, white daisies and narcissi, pink oleander and asphodels, blue mallows, gorse, and broom blanket the countryside. Private gardens run riot with daffodils, tulips, violets, jasmine, irises, roses, hibiscus, and geraniums. ✋ The Moroccan landscape varies dramatically. In the west, along the Atlantic shoreline, it is flat and agrarian, with acres of wheat and olive groves. In the north, on the Mediterranean, the verdant

A Berber motif decorates the striking narrow stairwell of this contemporary Marrakesh house.

Rif Mountains spill into the sea. Across the plain toward the south and down the middle of the country, the Atlas Mountains loom up against a brilliant blue sky, their caps snowcovered in winter. Southern Morocco is mostly desert, but the harsh, windswept, endless expanses do contain oases of date palms, fruit orchards, and roses. ✋ The story of Morocco begins with the Berbers, who are believed to have migrated originally from the Caucasus. Fair-skinned, often blue-eyed, Berbers comprise a significant part of Morocco's population. They arrived in the country around 1500 B.C. and developed major trade routes with the black kingdoms of West Africa. Some nomadic, others sedentary agriculturalists, the many hundreds of different patriarchal, polygamous Berber tribes—with their separate languages (only the Tuaregs of the Sahara have a written Berber language)—also traded with seafaring Phoenicians and Carthaginians who landed on the shores of what was then Mauritania. ✋ By the last century B.C. the Romans—who, incidentally, called the Berbers *Barbari*, hence "barbarian"—ruled Mauritania. Among the more noteworthy of Mauritania's governors was Juba II—noteworthy in the main for his marriage to Cleopatra Silene, daughter of Marc Antony and Cleopatra. In A.D. 683 there was a shift in power. An Arab army under the command of Oqba ben Nafi swept across Africa from the Near East. Settling in Morocco, these new conquerors introduced Islam as the religion of the

A tile roof is overgrown with weeds.

country, which they called *El Maghreb al Aqsa*, "The Land of the Far West." At the same time began a succession of Moroccan dynasties, among them the Idrisids, Almoravids, Almohads, Merinids, Saadians, and the current Alawites. With a base firmly established in Morocco, the Arabs were anxious to continue their attempt to convert the world to Islam. In A.D. 711 Tariq ibn Ziyad and his army of twelve thousand sailed across the Strait of Gibraltar from Morocco's Jabal Musa, one of the Pillars of Hercules, and began their conquest of Spain. ✋ During the eight hundred years the Arab Moroccans, or Moors, remained in Spain, additional Arabs continued to move into Morocco from the Near East. In A.D. 788 Moulay Idris, a descendant of the Prophet, and his followers fled there after defeat in battle near Mecca. In Morocco, he was accepted as ruler and forcefully persuaded the Berbers to convert from agrarian animism to Islam. Today, Berbers practice both animism and Islam. While the Arabs prospered in Morocco, the Moors were under constant attack from Spanish Christians and began to lose their control of southern Spain. They were forced out of Valencia in 1094, Zaragoza in 1118, Córdoba in 1236, and Seville in 1248. Finally, by 1492, when Ferdinand and Isabella captured Granada, the Moors were in full retreat back to Morocco. ✋ Morocco's extraordinarily large number of skilled artisans trace their father-to-son craftsmanship to this mass exodus of Andalusians who re-established their

Slender minarets rise from the roofscape of Fez.

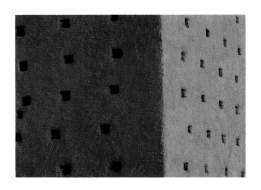

businesses on the North African side of the Strait of Gibraltar. Settling mostly in the four Imperial Cities—Fez, Marrakesh, Rabat, and Meknes—in a country never conquered by the Ottomans and therefore uniquely free from Turkish influences, these artisans introduced a distinct Hispano-Moorish style, one that continues to be purer and stronger than any found in other Arab nations today. ✋ By the beginning of the 18th century and throughout the 19th, adventurous Europeans were drawn to the exotic enchantment of North Africa. Often forced to camp for weeks outside a Moroccan city's walls before getting a local ruler's permission to enter, they were frequently rewarded by lavish and extended hospitality. Glowing descriptions in the diaries of intrepid travelers tell of courts where thousands of veiled women of the harem, rifle-bearing tribesmen, and turbaned slaves stumbled over one another to make the newcomers happy. According to Walter Harris, the London *Times* correspondent in Morocco at the turn of the 19th century, "compliments flowed as fast as mountain streams, happy in their wording, sonorous in their utterances, and absolutely insincere." ✋ Even at the turn of the 20th century Moroccans were engaged in fierce, long-standing intertribal warfare. Rich with sultanic intrigue, the country was medieval in many ways. The gates of Fez were closed at sunset each night, the walls of the city decorated with the cut-off heads of criminals displayed on spikes. ✋ The

Sunset turns the adobe walls of Marrakesh red.

Germans, the English, the French, and the Spanish all felt Morocco needed "protection," and each foreign nation sought to convince the sultan that it was the one to provide it. Finally Sultan Moulay Hafid agreed. Under attack and anxious for foreign aid, he signed the Treaty of Fez in 1912, giving the French the right to occupy southern Morocco and the Spanish the right to northern Morocco. ✋ The first resident-general (later marshal), Louis Lyautey, sought to pacify as well as to preserve the country during the French Protectorate. He was scrupulously careful not to undermine Islam or destroy any monuments and decreed that all new construction would be outside the ancient cities and kasbahs in the *Nouvelle Ville*, or New City. He was also instrumental in the building of the ports of Casablanca and Kenitra and saw to it that a modern educational system was introduced, government administration modernized, and the legal system reformed. Finally, during the Protectorate, peace was established among the feuding tribesmen. Cultivation of crops, vineyards, and cattle raising began. Roads and railroads were built. And phosphate, Morocco's major export, was discovered. ✋ By the 1950s and 1960s, Morocco's laissez-faire attitude toward foreign residents and their life-styles had become a magnet for many. Tangier in particular was a haven for hedonist, writer, and artist alike. Barbara Hutton, Paul Bowles, Elias Canetti, Joe Orton, Jean Genet, and William Burroughs were among the countless hundreds who

**Snow caps the
High Atlas Mountains
even in summer.**

were captivated by the mystery and hypnotic foreboding that the city and the rest of Morocco exuded. They found, too, that the country's paradoxical combination of vivid sensuality and intense spirituality—which was evident in the canvases of such artists as Eugène Delacroix, Théodore Géricault, and Henri Matisse, who painted in Morocco in the late-19th and early-20th centuries—still held strong. ✋ In 1956, during the reign of Mohammed V, Morocco gained independence from France and Spain. Today his grandson, Mohammed VI, is sovereign head of the Kingdom of Morocco. And despite increased tourism a good deal of the country remains miraculously and refreshingly removed from the rest of the world. ✋ Of special significance, traditional Moroccan architectural and artistic craftsmanship is flourishing. A major reason is that the current king's father, Hassan II, personally promoted the nation's ancient tradition of crafts. Anxious to keep Moroccan workers in gypsum and tile and painters of wood employed, Hassan II commissioned a magnificent mausoleum for his father in the capital, Rabat, and was responsible for the construction of the Hassan II mosque in Casablanca, recognized to be the finest example of contemporary Moroccan craftsmanship and perhaps one of the finest examples of Islamic design in the world. ✋ An estimated 2 million Moroccans, approximately 20 percent of the nation's working population, earn their livelihoods in craft production. Thou-

sands more, both men and women, are in government-sponsored craft schools. Rugs, the fourth major export, account for roughly 45 percent of all crafts in Morocco. Another 20 percent are leather crafts and 17 percent are ceramics and pottery. ✋ The mournful wail of a half dozen muezzins calling the faithful to prayer in Fez; the hoot of an owl, the song of a nightingale wafting through the orange-and-jasmine-perfumed air at the Hotel Gazelle d'Or in Taroudant; the red glow of sunset on the snowcovered High Atlas Mountains beyond the crenellated walls surrounding the garden at La Mamounia in Marrakesh—to travel in Morocco is a sensual, stimulating, tantalizing experience. ✋ So much to see. So much to buy. Handwoven baskets, olive jars, embroidery, hand-painted boxes, Berber jewelry, amulets, camel saddles, and rugs. The owners of the houses photographed for this book have had a great opportunity to search the souk when decorating their properties. They live in one of the world's most artistic nations. As guests in their homes, readers of this book are able to appreciate the skill and imagination these Moroccan and foreign homeowners have shown in using the nation's decorative arts and crafts in their houses' architecture and in furnishings.

Berber women cross the Sahara with fodder.

Palaces
Kasbahs and Ksour
Tents

Three Habitats

THREE TRADITIONAL WAYS IN WHICH PEOPLE CREATED PLACES TO live in Morocco bear witness to a remarkably varied geography. They testify as well to differing life-styles. ✋ City palaces conform to the Arab tradition of maintaining privacy. Exterior details were minimized lest they reveal the owner's wealth. Interiors, however, with striking tiled courtyards, were lavishly "furnished" with fabulous Moroccan craftsmanship. ✋ In the country stand ancient crenellated Berber kasbahs. Berbers pay special attention to the exterior decoration of their barely furnished dwellings and adorn their kasbahs' adobe exteriors with whitewashed motifs. ✋ In the Atlas and along the salt marshes bordering the Atlantic, Berber nomads pitch their tents. Multistriped and woven of animal hair, the tents are indistinguishable from the scorched earth of summer.

Perforations—outlined in white in the adobe wall and tower of a Berber kasbah in the southern Sahara—provide needed ventilation to kasbah interiors.

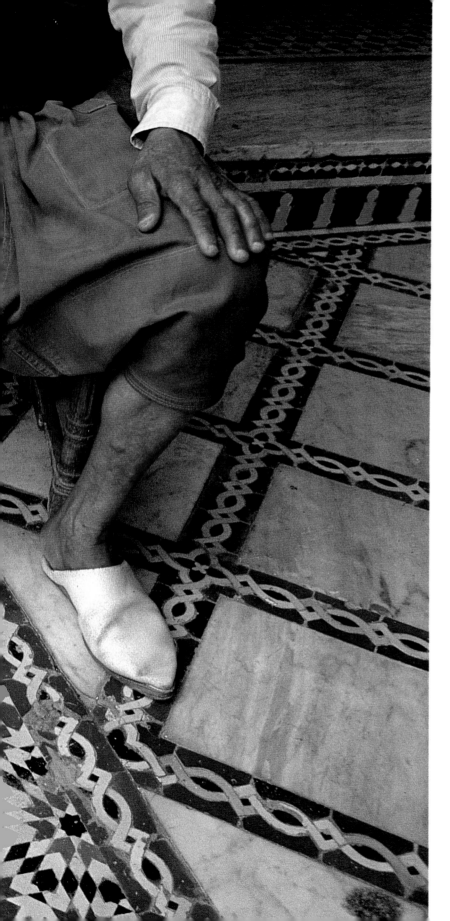

Palaces

VERY LARGE AND VERY SPLEN-
didly decorated—truly grand private houses more than anything—
Moroccan palaces were built and
lived in by monarchs and high
government officials as well as
wealthy merchants throughout
the country. It was in Fez, however, from the 16th through the
19th century, where Islamic palace architecture reached a pinna-
cle. The city's phenomenal wealth
and a local population of skilled
craftsmen led to the building of
some of the most elaborate and
luxurious palaces in the world.

As with all traditional building
in Morocco, absolute Islamic rules
of design prevailed. The "style"
of each palace was inevitably the
same: Hispano-Moorish. Differ-
ences lay in the number of rooms
and their degree of opulence.

**Fez is the location of the
Palais Mokri, built in
1910 for Tayeb Mokri.
The palace tiles come
from nearby kilns.**

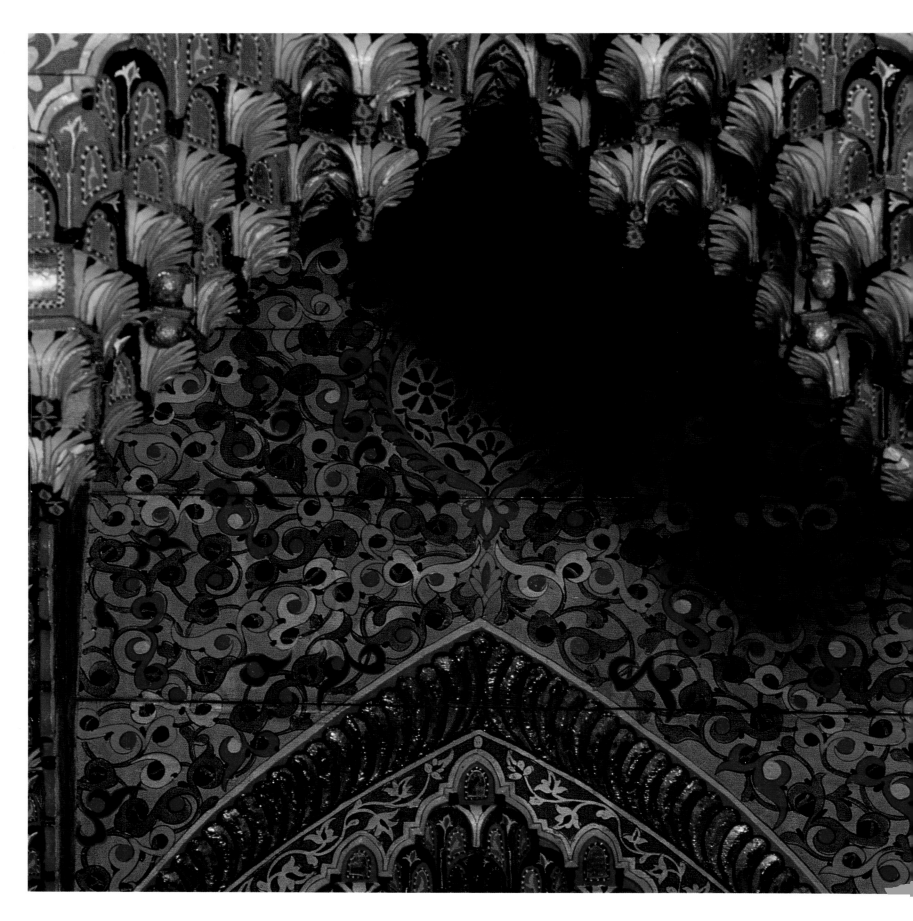

OPPOSITE: *zwaq,* or painting on wood, is common throughout Morocco. ABOVE: wrought-iron stairs and balustrades were imported from Italy. RIGHT: caid Tayeb Mokri once stood at the top of the grand staircase to welcome guests.

Still, there was some European influence. In the late 16th century, for example, Moroccan palace builders traded sugar for Italian marble that was carved into columns. And by the late 19th and early 20th centuries, a few palaces, including the Palais Mokri (built in 1910 by Tayeb Mokri), incorporated stained-glass windows, crystal chandeliers, even wrought-iron staircase balustrades shipped in from Europe.

As with European castles, many Moroccan palaces were too large and too expensive to maintain and ultimately were abandoned. Fortunately, some are being restored, including the 18th-century Palais Tazi in Fez, owned by the Benjelloun family.

The 19th-century Bahia palace in Marrakesh (built by Ba Ahmed, Vizier of Hassan I) has already been brought back to life.

A German Rud-Ibach-Sohn piano with a rare half-circular keyboard sits covered with years of dust in the music room of the Palais Mokri.

Its benefactor is King Mohammed VI, who moves frequently from one royal palace to another throughout the Imperial Cities of Rabat, Fez, Marrakesh, and Meknes.

Surrounded by massive gates and high walls, the royal palaces are huge; the royal palace in Fez, for instance, covers one hundred acres. In addition to *zelliges*, or tiles, they incorporate several "royal palace features," including *germuds*, or green tile roofs, and *jamurs*—roof spikes incorporating from one to five glistening brass balls of increasing size. *Jamurs* are frequently surmounted by the national emblem, the Moroccan star inside a crescent.

Palace building continues in Morocco. Under construction for more than ten years, His Majesty's residence in Agadir is reputed to contain the finest examples of modern-day Islamic design and craftsmanship in the kingdom, perhaps even in the world.

TOP: decorating a room, courtyard, or entrance with a succession of tile friezes of varying widths, patterns, and colors is common throughout Morocco. BOTTOM: modern tiles laid in age-old designs, traditional plasterwork, and calligraphy surround the doors of the royal palace in Fez.

The king's many palaces display the finest Moroccan craftsmanship, as seen in these enormous contemporary brass doors in Fez.

BOTH PAGES: the Bahia palace in Marrakesh is an example of 19th-century Andalusian-style domestic architecture. Of unusual significance is its undecorated, multicolored wooden ceiling, OPPOSITE, a rare example of beauty unadorned.

Kasbahs and Ksour

BERBER STRONGHOLDS DATING from the 14th century, Moroccan kasbahs, monumental single-family fortresses, and ksour, fortified tribal villages, are dramatically located on plateaus towering over fertile valleys planted with fruit trees and grain. Kasbahs are especially conspicuous along the Dras, Dades, Todrha, and Tafilat river valleys on the eastern slopes of the Atlas Mountains; on the edges of date palm oases bordering the Sahara; and along what is commonly called the Route of the Kasbahs between the desert towns of Er-Rachidia and Quarzazate.

Built of *pisé,* or pounded red earth reinforced with straw, kasbahs with their enormous wooden gates and walled ksour appear like

BOTH PAGES: only occasionally visited by its owners, who live in Casablanca, this adobe kasbah in the highly decorated village of Amerhidl in the southern Sahara is slowly beginning to crumble.

gigantic mirages against brilliant blue horizons. Unlike discreet Arab town houses of the north, with their plain exteriors and hidden luxurious interiors built around courtyards, kasbahs willingly show their faces to the world, with adobe exteriors that are often embellished with bold, geometric Berber motifs incised or painted in white. Inside, however, kasbahs and ksour are honeycombs of dark, narrow passageways leading to lookout points, grain rooms, and animal shelters. Here there are no fine painted ceilings or tiles.

Once stopover points for camel caravans going through the great Tizi n'Tishka and Tizi n'Test passes of the High Atlas Mountains en route to Timbuktu to trade for gold, amber, ostrich feathers, and animal skins, many kasbahs and ksour are empty today. They are windswept, sandblasted, and fast turning to ruins.

This 19th-century ksar, Ait Benhaddou, is near Quarzazate in the southern Sahara. It has appeared as a location in several epic films, including *Lawrence of Arabia*.

Tents

BERBER SHEPHERDS LIVE IN TENTS when they take their sheep to pasture in the Atlas Mountains or along the salt marshes on the Atlantic and Mediterranean coastlines. Upon arrival at a campsite, the men drive the first peg, or *adriq*, into the ground. The women then set up the tent, dividing it in two; one side for themselves, the other for the men and important visitors. Finally, herbs are scattered on the ground inside the tent to ensure protection and prosperity.

Moroccan *flij*, or tent strips, are usually sixty centimeters wide and are clamped or sewn together. Handwoven from sheep wool and goat hair, tent material is predominantly black and brown, with shadings of beige, tan, and off-white. From a distance, and in

LEFT: each spring, thousands of tribesmen pitch *makhzens*, or festival tents, outside the royal palace in Marrakesh to honor the king on Throne Day. OPPOSITE: traditional Berber tents are made of strips handwoven from sheep wool and goat hair.

ABOVE: *makhzens* are lined with *ha'iti*, or wall coverings, made of strips of appliquéd fabric that are pieced together.
LEFT: upon arrival at a campsite, Berber men drive the first peg, or *adriq*, into the ground.

149-6 1 3

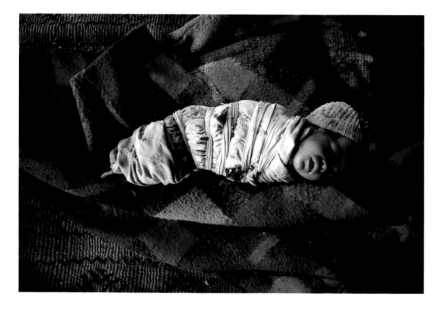

summer especially Moroccan tents often blend in with the parched, rugged landscape, becoming totally camouflaged. Inside, dozens of rugs are laid out on the floor and stacked in piles six to ten feet high. Large, textured pillows are strewn about for sitting and sleeping.

Makhzens, or festival tents, are traditionally put up in the countryside by chiefs for their personal use during important tribal gatherings and other special events. Made from heavy white canvas, these caidal tents are usually decorated outside with black leather depicting crenellation and *qandils*, or oil lamps.

On Throne Day each spring, dozens of *makhzens* are set up in the campground outside the Marrakesh palace of King Mohammed VI. Members of the court, visitors, and foreign dignitaries are entertained at lavish banquets

TOP: rugs are hung from the sides on Berber tents as insulation. CENTER: wrapped tightly in swaddling bands, a Berber baby sleeps on a handwoven blanket. BOTTOM: wool embroidery often decorates Berber tents.

ABOVE: a Berber tent, purchased by a city dweller, has been lavishly decorated for a party. RIGHT: the primitive charcoal stove is used both for heat and cooking. OPPOSITE: made of heavy-duty canvas, *makhzens* are decorated on the outside with *qandil*, black leather motifs that symbolize oil lamps.

inside the tents. Outside, tribesmen stage *fantasias* throughout the day. As many as two dozen tribesmen will gallop across the field in a straight line, pull their horses to an abrupt stop, raise their rifles into the air, and fire in dramatic unison.

Today people living in Moroccan cities often buy Berber shepherd and caidal tents to put in their gardens for parties.

York Castle

YORK CASTLE HAS STOOD GUARD OVER TANGIER FOR FIVE centuries, like a watchman in the night. High on a promontory on the Place de la Kasbah, the fortress looms over the city's eyeblinding, whitewashed houses and harbor below. ✋ Anyone standing on its large, crenellated terraces can see from North Africa to Europe across the Strait of Gibraltar. Leaving the Atlantic to enter the Mediterranean, captains look up at the landmark, which passed from the occupying British to the native Moors in 1684. ✋ The Phoenicians were the first to settle in Tangier in the 4th century BC and it has since been occupied by the Romans and the Portuguese, but it was under the English that York Castle was built. Like the Barbary pirates who once lurked behind its massive walls, the fortress has earned an international reputation, making it one of Tangier's

Tangier is more cosmopolitan than it is Moroccan. A still-life arrangement in York Castle reflects this international perspective by its artful combination of Chinese coral, Islamic pottery, Indian bronze, and English dinnerware.

leading landmarks. Gray and forbidding on the outside, the fortress-turned-habitat is cheerful, colorful and cozy on the inside. The talents behind this astounding transformation from ruins to splendor are the castle's occupants Yves Vidal retired president of Knoll International France and designer Charles Sevigny, who commute between Tangier and their Parisian apartment.

"When I saw the castle in 1961, no one wanted it. It was a disaster. There was no roof, no doors, no windows." Working with Belgian architect Robert Gerofi,

ABOVE: Dating from the 16th century, York Castle overlooks the entrance to the Mediterranean. RIGHT: One of the castle's many terraces offers views down over the all-white city. The embroidered black-and-white pillow fabric is from Fez.

LEFT: Knoll furniture is a clue to Yves Vidal's one-time French presidency of the company. The woven rattan rug is a traditional Moroccan floor covering. ABOVE: Reclining on a sumptuous array of brightly colored cushions, guests look out across the Strait of Gibraltar to Spain.

responsible for the reconstruction of Malcolm Forbes's Tangier villa, Vidal and Sevigny created one of the best-known historic restorations in North Africa. Today, guests are entertained in rooms whose eclectic style is historically appropriate in a city with a multinational heritage that continues to draw visitors and new residents from around the world.

LEFT: Antique, hand-painted doors display age-old Moorish patterns. Many of the ceramic pieces are contemporary. **ABOVE:** Window grills throughout Morocco are of fanciful design and allow protection, as well as providing air circulation.

LEFT: Designer Charles Sevigny combines an Indian bedspread, a Persian mirror and a Moroccan jar in a guest bedroom.
BELOW LEFT: Many rooms in York Castle look straight out over the Atlantic.
BELOW RIGHT: Dinner guests are entertained under a tent festooned with Moroccan lanterns.
RIGHT: Surrounding a *riyad,* courtyard, public rooms have multiple purposes: afternoon tea, dining, card playing.

Chaouen

In Chaouen, Rif
mountain women often
use handwoven textiles as
padding to balance
heavy loads.

PERCHED ON THE SIDE OF A DEEP RAVINE IN THE REMOTE, RUGGED Rif Mountains in northern Morocco, the village of Chaouen (Chechaouen) was founded in 1480 by Arab prince Ali ibn Rachid. Here, Muslims and Jews, fleeing Spain and Christian persecution, held out against repeated attacks. Chaouen also became a pilgrimage destination for Berber followers of Moulay Abdessalam ben Mchich. Patron saint of the local Djhebali tribesmen, he is buried in the nearby countryside. ✋ Off-limits to non-Muslims for centuries and only finally conquered by the Spanish in 1926 at the time of the Protectorate, Chaouen today welcomes visitors. They are immediately struck by the town's roofs, which are tiled and eaved, in contrast to the flat roofs found throughout the rest of Morocco, and speak of Chaouen's Andalusian heritage. Unspoiled because of years of isolation,

Chaouen has a shimmering "lunar" atmosphere. As if one continuous surface molded from plastic, stone walls, alcoves, Moorish arches, interior courtyards, and narrow cobbled streets are covered with whitewash that has been tinted a luminous, bone-chilling blue. Some say the color frightens mosquitoes away, others that it reduces the glare of the brilliant, high-altitude sunlight.

Here Spanish is heard more often than French and city life seems of another time. Black-eyed, olive-skinned housewives make furtive excursions, scurrying through aquamarine-colored, grottolike alleys to the fruit and vegetable market and the local bakery. Children kick balls and skip rope in front of studded bright blue doors. And old women lead donkeys in from the countryside with a nighttime supply of firewood from the nearby forests.

Moroccan exterior doors-within-doors allow homeowners both privacy and protection. They are opened only as long as needed—for a visitor, a pack mule, a large delivery.

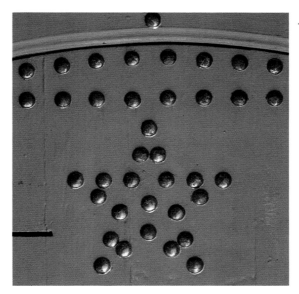

A study in color and texture. Exteriors of houses are painted a bone-chilling blue. Doors are often studded in star patterns. Courtyards are swept clean with brushes. Pom-poms decorate traditional hats worn by Rif mountain women, who bring fodder into town each evening.

RIGHT: open-back *babouches,* or heelless slippers, are taken off before entering a Moroccan house. Men prefer plain colors— yellow for everyday, white to go to the mosque. Women's *babouches* are many colored and gaily embroidered. OPPOSITE: striped wool fabrics are often hung to air outside doorways.

TOP: Moroccan housewives take homemade bread dough to the nearest communal oven for baking. ABOVE: lace hangs in the deep window of a Chaouen house. OPPOSITE: Berber women pass the decorated entrance to a mosque.

A Rif Mountain Retreat

Designer Jean Lou
Guerin prepares tea on a
gas burner in his
courtyard kitchen.
Couscous platters rest
against the terra-cotta-
colored walls. Floor tiles
are Spanish.

CHAOUEN DOESN'T READILY ACCEPT STRANGERS. IT TOOK JEAN LOU Guerin several years to convince his Berber landlord to rent him a 150-year-old, three-story property tucked away in an alley. Once there, he made it his own. ✋ "For me, the things of the spirit, not the things of a house, are what count," he confides. "That's why there's so little in my house." ✋ Indeed, a few decorative pots, hand-woven bedspreads, tables, and chairs comprise the house's "furnish-ings." Flour sacks stretched out on strings serve as sun shields. ✋ "Unlike locals in Chaouen, whose houses are primarily whitewashed inside, I added colors to the lye," Guerin says, motioning to the vibrant greens, rusts, pinks, and blues of walls, columns, and stairs. On the outside, he conforms to tradition and repaints several times a year with Chaouen's signature iceberg blue.

ABOVE: a steep flight of stairs with black-and-white Spanish tiles and melon-colored walls leads to the second floor. OPPOSITE: a storage and laundry room. The mottled effect is produced by the house's damp walls.

OPPOSITE: Guerin's strong artistic color sense is evident throughout the 150-year-old house. Each room is a different color. ABOVE: the house is built around a traditional Moroccan *riyad*, or courtyard, paved with brilliant tile. LEFT: prototypes for Guerin's colorful leatherwork. Made in his workshop, they are exported worldwide.

RIGHT: handwoven, black-and-white Berber material covers a cot. A goat-hide floor covering and a basketful of kindling complete the guest room furnishings. OPPOSITE, FROM TOP: a wood-burning stove heats the house in winter; the stool is made of cork. Guerin's courtyard workbench is covered with leathercraft tools. In a bedroom, a Berber carpet hangs over the bed and a Berber straw-and-wool rug covers the floor.

A Touch of Spain

An old wooden chair is painted a striking flamenco red. Black-and-white floor tiles are from Spain. The red-and-white handwoven, wool material is a *courzya*, or apron, worn by local Berber women.

LONDON ART DEALER MICHAEL PARKINS, HIS WIFE, AND CHILDREN vacation in an eighty-year-old house in Chaouen. Inaccessible by car but only minutes by foot from Place Mohammed V with its crafts vendors and fruit and vegetable stalls, the *dar*, or house, is a classic example of Hispano-Moorish design whose Andalusian roots date to the 14th century. ✋ With its windowless outside walls built straight up from the street like a rampart, the Parkinses' hideaway typifies the age-old Moroccan homeowner's belief that conspicuous exteriors are a poor show. ✋ As in other Arab countries, a traditional Moroccan home is more than a place to live. It is a private enclosure for contemplation, an oasis away from the outside world. For centuries, isolation and intimacy have remained important to Moroccan homeowners. What is inside is nobody's business except the owner's.

RIGHT: A steep inside staircase leads down from the rooms surrounding a courtyard. OPPOSITE: like many foreigners, the Parkinses use Rif Mountains materials for decorating their house.

On the ground floor, the Parkinses' long, narrow, arcaded reception rooms open onto tiled *wust ed dar*, which allows maximum indoor-outdoor living. A staircase leads to upstairs bedrooms and additional living rooms that face the corridors overlooking the courtyard.

RIGHT: the souk in Quezzane near Chaouen is full of shops selling brightly colored, handpainted chests like this one. OPPOSITE: the Parkinses' second-floor bedrooms face onto a *riyad;* interior doors and windows admit air and light.

Strong primary colors are the principal decoration of the sparsely furnished house. The handwoven striped wool spread was bought in the souk.

ABOVE: the antique chest and shelf are from Tétouan.
RIGHT: two Berber-style plaster arches flank an Islamic arch, separating a ground-floor courtyard from the main reception room. A *haiti,* cut-out material sewn together to decorate the inside of a tent, is hung on the wall. Local handwoven material covers two couches and the banquettes. A bouquet of fresh mint sits on a table.

Textiles
Rugs
Leather
Pottery
Thuya Wood

Folk Arts

LIKE THE BERBERS, EARLY ARABS LIVED IN TENTS WITH FURNISHINGS that were utilitarian and able to be strapped to a horse or camel. They may not have been luxury items, but tremendous skill went into their making. ✋ Inspired by former king Hassan II, Moroccans have a renewed appreciation of their Berber and Islamic traditions. Hassan II triggered a renaissance in the country's arts and crafts, many of which trace their Hispano-Moorish origins to the Moors' flight from Spain in the 15th century. ✋ Blessed with ample artisans who can produce custom-made furniture and accessories at a fraction of what it would cost in Europe or the United States, Moroccans frequently commission all the furnishings for their houses. Although many modern-day Moroccans have European furniture in their houses, it is almost always combined with their own country's arts and crafts.

Homeowners in Morocco frequently decorate with antique rugs from North Africa and the Near East, which they turn into wall art.

Textiles

FOR CENTURIES, MOROCCANS and Berbers have produced a rich variety of textiles, many of which are embroidered. Different styles of historic Moroccan and Berber textiles are easily recognized by collectors. Rabat workmanship is solid and robust. Fez is known for its delicate, aesthetic sense. Meknes textiles are heavy and primitive. Curious symbols representing exotic birds, dragons, and chimera are found in textiles from the seaport of Salé and from the trade route centers of Tétouan and Azemmour—evidence of exposure to patterns from Europe and central Africa.

Although local mills, particularly in Fez, now mass-produce textiles in both traditional and contemporary designs, most Moroccans continue to dress in hand-woven—and handmade—cloth-

Women in Essaouira dress in all-white, -black, or -brown *haiks*, or robes, and wear veils. When visiting outside, they face a wall to avoid eye contact with men and strangers.

ing. Women are particularly proud of their caftans, which are made throughout the country in thousands of all-male caftan workshops. Men wear *djellabas*, or robes. In winter, they also wear *burnooses*, or woolen cloaks.

Embroidery on sophisticated silk brocades and on the more prosaic linens and wools was the work of young women, usually for their trousseaus. Unlike European and American samplers, this work was never signed. But the woman could express individuality through her interpretation of the traditional motifs: stars, rosettes, the hand of Fatima, tulips, narcissus, cypress trees, scorpions, centipedes—even lice. They could also personalize their handiwork by their choice of colors. Silk threads of mauve, blue, gray, brown, and black make up the Moroccan palette; Berber

ABOVE: silk-embroidered
wedding belts from Fez
are prized by collectors.
RIGHT: women dancers
wear dresses from
the Sahara at the annual
Festival of the Rose
in El-Kelaa-des-Mgouna.

Machine-made textiles
are often used as coverings for
pillows sold in the souk.

Moroccan textiles used for
clothing and for interior
design range in color
from subtle to vibrant, in design
from naive to sophisticated.
Here is part of Morocco's
bounty: rugs airing
high in the Atlas Mountains,
contemporary pillows
displayed in a Marrakesh
salon, yard goods for sale in
the Chaouen souk.

The unusual wool wall hangings and rugs above were designed by textile collector Bert Flint. Spools of fine silk are sold in the Fez souk. A living room outside of Essaouira is decorated with traditional fabrics. Costumed stick figures are displayed by women during a festival in Marrakesh.

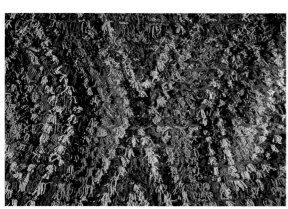

needleworkers often opted for cotton or wool threads of brilliant reds, yellows, and purples.

Today, it is in interior design where the use of textiles in Morocco is being rethought. There is movement toward a more livable, relaxed look, especially in Marrakesh. Both in the medina and outside town, homeowners are using traditional country textiles for bedspreads, curtains, and upholstery. They prowl souks in search of colorful striped Berber wools from the mountains near Chaouen; off-white, nubbly, couscous-textured cottons from Essaouira; and rough-textured wools and cottons in a desert-toned brown from Taroudant.

OPPOSITE: Moroccan textiles worn as clothing frequently clash in pattern and color. ABOVE: inspiration for colors in Moroccan fabrics is found in the country's infinite variety of wildflowers, which are frequently found in bundles of fresh-cut grass used to feed livestock.

Rugs

FOR HUNDREDS OF YEARS AMID the cedar forests and snowbound valleys of the Atlas Mountains, in the shadow of crenellated walls of Saharan kasbahs, and along the labyrinthian alleyways of urban medinas, Moroccan women have woven rugs.

Appreciated for their exciting color combinations and often distinctive designs, Moroccan rugs are divided into two categories: rural and urban. Rural rugs are further identified by region, then by tribe (of which there are over five hundred in Morocco). For the

ABOVE: a vendor in Essaouira shows wool yarn to a potential buyer. RIGHT: ask to see a rug and you'll be shown a hundred at the Bazaar du Sud in Marrakesh.

most part, rural rugs are striped, although stylized motifs inspired by ancient symbols or strong imaginations are not uncommon. Rugs from Rehamna and Chiadma are as abstract as paintings by Jackson Pollock or Piet Mondrian; they are especially prized for their distinctive weave and colors that range from subtle earth tones to brilliant saffrons, beryls, and crimsons.

Urban rugs are made mainly in

OPPOSITE: in Fez, wool dyeing has been done by hand—and by feet—for hundreds of years by the same families in the souk. **ABOVE LEFT:** white wool yarn will be turned into a thick pile rug at a weaving collective in Sidi-Moktar. All-white rugs are mainly exported to Europe. **ABOVE:** synthetic dyes are popular today and produce rugs with colors verging on neon. **LEFT:** on "Throne Day" the king and his entourage will drive over these Rabat rugs spread out on the streets of Marrakesh.

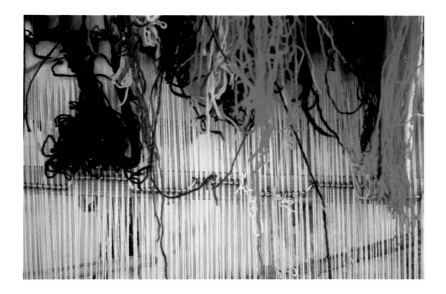

Rabat and Mediouna and have a more formal design than rural carpets. Easily recognizable by their palette of vivid oranges, sunset reds, spring greens, and soft mauves, they frequently have a large center field covered with octagonal medallions. Motifs include flowers, teapots, toads, palm trees, and mules.

Berber rugs have strong geometric designs and often combine thick pile and flat weave. Less expensive, though popular with folk art collectors, are Berber mats. These are woven from dwarf palm or esperato grass with decorative designs woven into them in wool most often in shades of red.

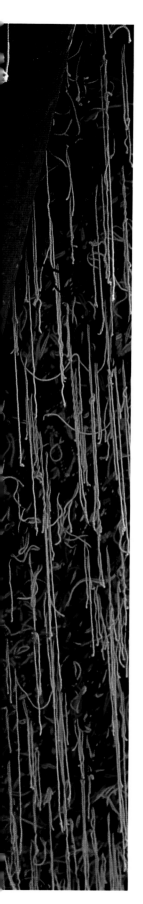

OPPOSITE: less expensive and increasingly appreciated, Berber rugs made out of dwarf palm or esperato grass reproduce decorative designs popular in wool. Long uncut vegetable fibers along their backs serve as a natural cushion. These rugs also cover walls for winter warmth. CENTER: fringe on many contemporary rugs is often simply the result of weavers leaving floating waft threads uncut. LEFT: a merchant displays rugs for sale at the Bazaar du Sud in Marrakesh.

Almost all Moroccan rugs are stamped by government officials with color-coded labels for quality. The wool used must be spun from fleece and the colors made from colorfast dyes. As for value: "We look for the originality of the weaver," explains Moulay Charif, owner of the well-known Bazaar du Sud rug store in Marrakesh. "Repetition of design in a rug lowers the price. Spontaneity and creativity in weaving raises it." When selling, weavers turn to

OPPOSITE: to go into a rug shop in Morocco is to be served endless glasses of mint tea. With each rug pulled down from the stacks at Ali Babi in Taroudant, another glass of tea is poured. ABOVE: in Marrakesh, a rug merchant displays his wares on an alley wall.

runners working the countryside or sell directly at a rug auction.

Shoppers with sufficient stamina may test their mettle at a rug shop, where multiple rounds of mint tea will accompany the fifty, seventy-five, even as many as one hundred rugs spread out at one's feet. Experienced buyers counsel that one must bargain hard, beware of nylon threads passing for silk, and deal only with reputable shopkeepers. *Caveat emptor.*

BELOW: rare antique Berber rugs are appreciated for the many symbolic patterns and designs woven into them. OPPOSITE: like abstract paintings, Berber rugs, such as this one in the Bert Flint collection, are often nonrepresentational.

Leather

WITH THE RETURN OF THE MOORS from Spain in the 15th century, Fez became the center of the leather industry. The expertise of its tanners and bookbinders made the word "Morocco" synonymous throughout the Western world with fine leather. Still today, Fez is the center of the Moroccan leather industry.

Visitors to Fez climb up slippery, narrow stairs in Dabbaghin, the section of the souk where the tanneries are located. From rooftops, and holding bouquets of mint to minimize the awful stench, they look down upon a medieval scene. Hundreds of men stand calf-deep in honeycombed vats full of chemical dyes and cow urine—only a few tanneries continue to use bark and plant pigments. The workers' bare legs

OPPOSITE: in Fez, cowhides, camelskins, and goatskins are spread out to dry after dyeing. LEFT, FROM TOP: skins are washed, scraped, and soaked for several days to soften them. Leather is often painted after it is dyed. What isn't exported or turned into *babouches* may be sold in the souk.

vary in color from yellow, red, and blue to green and black—the result of treading on cowhides, goatskins, and camelskins for up to twelve hours a day.

The finished skins are rubbed with wooden blocks to remove wrinkles, dried in the sun, and then stacked and tied in bunches according to size and quality. Moroccan leather is a multimillion-dollar export. What remains in the country is turned into *babouches* (hand-embroidered slippers), hassocks, bags, belts, and saddles.

Yellow *babouches* are traditional Moroccan leather slippers worn by men.

Pottery

THE HISTORY OF MOROCCAN pottery dates back a thousand years. However, it was in the 15th century when the craft truly became important. Moors skilled in pottery fled Spain for Morocco and settled in Fez, Meknes, Safi, and Marrakesh. Here they rebuilt their kilns. And for the next four centuries, Moroccan potters, particularly those in Fez, prospered and produced some of the finest examples of their trade in the Islamic world.

By the beginning of the 20th century, however, the quality of Moroccan pottery had diminished. The importation of mass-produced pottery from Europe reduced the incentive of Moroccan potters to practice their skills.

A renaissance of the centuries-old Moroccan pottery industry

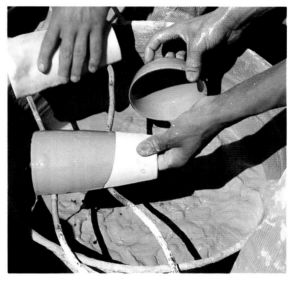

OPPOSITE: in Safi, 1920s-style vases are made for export. Their simplicity and strong colors are popular in Europe. LEFT, FROM TOP: Moroccan potters soften clay by foot before shaping it by hand. Roof tiles are dyed by hand. Jars wait to be fired in a kiln in Safi.

occurred during the French Protectorate. Anxious to introduce Moroccan craftsmanship to the European market, the resident-general, Louis Lyautey, sent Moroccan potters to Sèvres in France to learn new techniques. Examples of their rekindled skill were introduced at the Fez Fair in 1916. The local as well as European markets were quick to support the new work.

Today, thousands of Moroccan

ABOVE LEFT: a Saharan water jar decorates the entrance to a private house in the medina in Marrakesh. ABOVE: a worker at the Safi kilns carries clay. LEFT: a jar is nestled in a blanket for display.

Pottery is displayed
at dozens of street stalls
that line the street
leading to the Safi kilns.

potters pound clay, spin wheels, and shape the myriad bowls, vases, and dishes that continue to be made in the country's historic pottery centers.

Traditional Andalusian-inspired, polychrome enameled pottery made in Fez is the most respected in Morocco. It is blue and white for the most part, though yellow, green, white, black, and brown glazes are also common. Fez pottery dinner plates, *jebana*, or butter jars, carafes, pitchers, vases, perfume jars, and inkstands are found in shops throughout the country.

Fakhkhari Hamida et Fils is a major pottery workshop on the outskirts of Fez. Here the division of labor continues in the same way it has in the pottery trade for centuries. A dozen young male apprentices race from station to station, carrying different items to the older men who spin the potting wheels and stoke and pack

the kilns. At this particular workshop, women design and trace intricate traditional Islamic patterns onto the pieces of pottery.

Pottery buffs also enjoy visiting Safi to see the country's oldest kilns. Located on Potters' Hill, they are more than two hundred years old and still in operation. Here, potters produce fanciful, repetitive designs on turquoise, white, and cream-colored backgrounds.

Polychrome glazed pottery

OPPOSITE: two 19th-century Fez polychromed enamel dishes rest against a painted 19th-century wood panel. ABOVE: roof tiles are laid out to dry in the sun.

119

made in Meknes is the most widely distributed in Morocco. It is sold in souks and at roadside stands everywhere.

Unlike Europe, where many ceramics were made for decoration and to show off the skill of their makers, Moroccan pottery has always been utilitarian. This explains why so many pieces of Moroccan pottery are nicked and chipped. It also explains why there are so few genuine antique pieces of Moroccan pottery in existence today.

Rahalia, large Moroccan plates from Fez, made strictly for wall decoration, are an exception; many are truly old. So are decorated Saharan and Berber terracotta ware: olive oil jugs, milk and water pots, oil lamps, teapots, and animal figures. Like all examples of fine Moroccan pottery, they, too, are now sought by collectors worldwide.

FROM TOP: a street sign directs customers to "Potters' Hill" in Safi. Written in Arabic and French, the sign summarizes the recent history of Morocco. Nineteenth-century *jebanas,* or butter pots, are occasionally found in antique shops. Rimmed in copper to prevent them from chipping, bichrome bowls are made by Fakhkhari Hamida et Fils in Fez. OPPOSITE: a shipment of antiques for export to a retail outlet in Santa Fe, New Mexico, includes oil storage jars from Taroudant.

Thuya Wood

THUYA TREES RESEMBLE SCRUB oaks and are native to the flat, sandy countryside outside Essaouira on the Atlantic shoreline. The short, scruffy trees are valued for the extraordinary beauty of their wood, which ranges in color from dark mahogany brown to subtle buff. Thuya may be all one color, all one grain; or it may be burled, with an explosion of grains and varying hues.

Danish designer, collector, and gallery owner Frederic Damgaard restored a 150-year-old house in Essaouira. He entertains friends at his antique mother-of-pearl and thuya-wood tables.

The popularity of thuya reached its height during the French Protectorate. And because many Europeans were living in Morocco, thuya bureaus, armoires, tables, and chairs made there in the early 20th century reflected European taste.

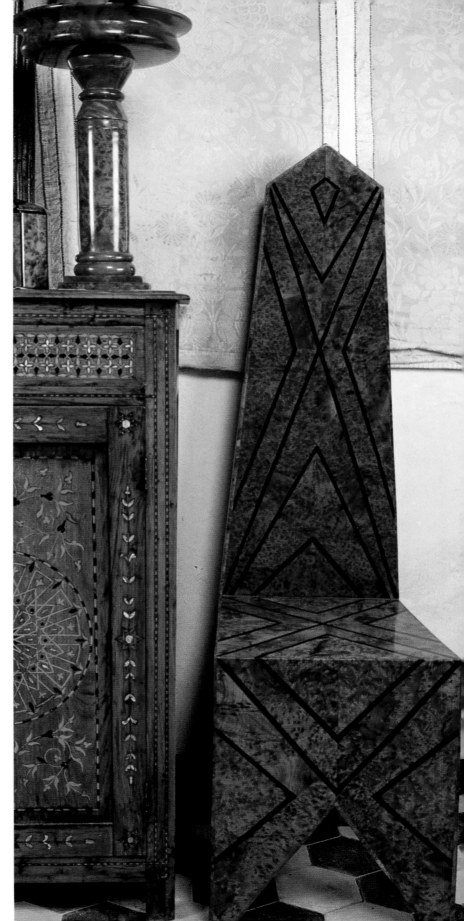

Today, hundreds of wood-workers in Essaouira spend twelve-hour days inside ateliers under miles of arcades that line the narrow streets of the blue-shuttered, all-white seaport. Skilled in marquetry, they finalize their handicrafts by rubbing the boxes, chess sets, tables, chairs, picture frames, and jewelry for hours with small cotton balls soaked in vegetable oil, bringing out the wood's patina. Workshop entrances are piled high with thuya wood ready to be worked. And dozens of crates of finished items wait for delivery to Moroccan souks or shipment abroad.

Casablanca Deco

WHAT NEW YORK CITY IS TO THE UNITED STATES, CASABLANCA IS to Morocco: a crowded, noisy, wealthy, commercial center on the Atlantic coast. The North African metropolis is surprisingly unappreciated, both at home and abroad, for its unique abundance of Art Deco architecture. ✋ Once a sleepy, out-of-the-way fishing village, Casablanca blossomed under the French Protectorate and became a boom town with a first-class port. Along its wide, palm-lined boulevards luxurious Art Deco apartment and office buildings reminiscent of the Trocadero district in Paris sprang up. ✋ Today, Casablanca city officials are anxious to establish an Art Deco historic district. Efforts are under way to rekindle public appreciation of the city's dazzling collection of building facades, front doors, balconies, and balustraded staircases from the increasingly popular 1920s and 1930s.

Downtown Casablanca attracts apartment dwellers who want to live in Art Deco buildings with fanciful, all-white facades and wrought-iron balconies.

Rhythmic Art Deco designs
with floral, bird, animal, and
abstract geometric
motifs, influenced by European
and Islamic traditions, are seen
throughout Casablanca.
Art Deco wrought-iron windows,
staircases, and balconies—
as well as stuccoed
pediments and friezes—
punctuate the city.

129

Landmark Villa

HOME FOR MORE THAN SIXTY YEARS OF THE LEGENDARY COUNTESS de Breteuil, the Hispano-Moorish Villa Taylor is in the middle of Marrakesh yet hidden from public view. It lies today behind massive, guarded gates in an enormous garden of palm, fir, and olive trees.

🖐 A superb example of lavish, massive, pre–World War II Moroccan architecture and interior design—the house was built in the 1920s—the villa's huge main rooms contain museum-quality handpainted ceilings, doors, and shutters. "Scholars come here all the time to study the craftsmanship," says the countess. 🖐 With many cozy, secluded small rooms in towers up hidden staircases, perfect for têtes-à-têtes or *liaisons amoureuses*, the villa is best known for the splendor and richness of its Moroccan-tiled living room, where visitors step back in time. Tigerskin rugs, deep sofas piled with pillows covered in

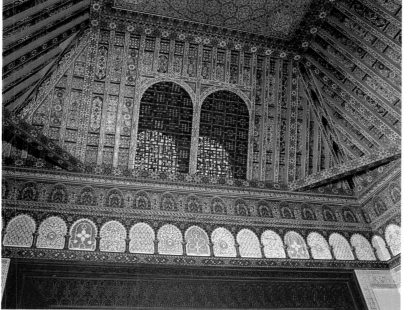

Moroccan fabrics, big leather ottomans, a shortwave radio picking up jazz beamed in from Paris, tables crowded with family photographs in silver frames and vases of pink and red roses from the garden: *le grand salon* is a marvelous continuation of French Protectorate *luxe* life-style in Morocco. Here, for years, the countess has entertained scores of friends beneath a towering, sumptuous green-and-yellow Marrakesh-style wood ceiling. Painted with *zwags*, floral and geometric motifs, it is made—as is all paneling in Morocco—from rotproof and wormproof Atlas Mountain

FAR LEFT: a massive front door opens onto a foyer. ABOVE LEFT: a brass door bell is placed in the center of a hand of Fatima—a talisman against the evil eye. LEFT AND OPPOSITE: in the *grand salon*, under an enormous painted wood ceiling, hangs an 18th-century ancestor portrait of Gabrielle Emilie de Breteuil, Marquise du Chatalet.

cedar, which doesn't need to be treated or varnished. True to tradition, the lower part of the wall is covered with a panel of *zelliges*, the upper portion with a frieze of very finely carved plaster of Paris windows, or *chems*.

An ancient bell system still serves a purpose in the rambling three-story villa. When the signal under the word "Madame" flashes, it usually signifies that it is time to take the countess her breakfast tray. Bells labeled "Chambre Rouge," "Chambre Jaune," and "Chambre Bleu" summon the staff to eight guest rooms, each with a different Moroccan motif, a sunken marble bathtub, well-worn rugs, and a fireplace. "Loge" is the wood-paneled card room. And "Secret" (for "*Secrétaire*") is the library, where Winston Churchill and Franklin Roosevelt sat down for further talks after the Casablanca

Painted wood doors are juxtaposed with multicolored tiles in a guest bedroom. The different types of craftsmanship throughout Villa Taylor are superb examples of the numerous decorative elements found in private houses and palaces in Morocco.

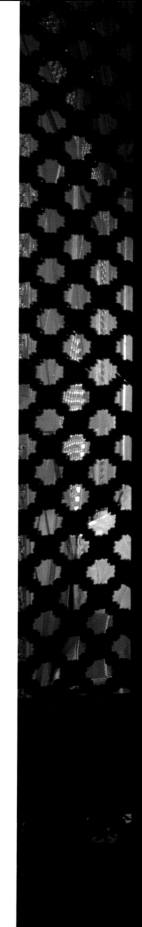

ABOVE: different color
themes give identity
to the villa's guest
rooms. RIGHT: breakfast
trays await delivery by
the staff each morning
in the courtyard.

Conference in January of 1943.

"Churchill was so moved by the sight of the snow-capped Atlas from the villa roof, he persuaded the president to allow himself to be taken out of his wheelchair and carried up," the countess recalls. "It was dusk. The mountains were blood red and the muezzins had begun to call the faithful to prayer. It was one of the deepest moments in the two friends' lives."

Today, the Countess de Breteuil climbs the same three staircases up to her roof several times a day, alone. From morning until evening, she has never grown tired of her view. *"C'est ma promenade,"* she says, and smiles.

Unpainted wood, seen in this jewel-like cedar *petit salon* inset with *moucharaby* panels, is uncommon in Morocco. Rural weavings and leather pillows give a Saharan atmosphere to the room.

A Moroccan Folly

U.S. AMBASSADOR TO MOROCCO FREDERICK VREELAND, AND HIS wife, artist Vanessa Somers, once lived in Rome. But they vacationed in Marrakesh, where they have built, are still building, and insist they will always be building Villa Cafrevan in the Palmeraie, or palm oasis. Inside and out, it is a blend of Indian, Moroccan, Italian, and 1001 Nights architecture whose unconventionality has amazed all of Marrakesh for years. 🖐 The rambling, adobe fun house, designed by French solar architect Dominic Michelis, is multileveled and contains endless grand salons, petits salons, nooks, crannies, grottoes, staircases, landings, hideaways, and balconies. There are eight theme bedrooms—Jungle, Bonsai, Nursery, and Tantra among them—and twelve baths. 🖐 Surrounded by acres of palms, umbrella pines from Italy, litchi trees from China, and mango trees from Florida, the

villa's first non-Moroccan surprise is a columned entryway. It is a replica of Borromini's famed trompe l'oeil loggia in the Palazzo Spada in Rome. "Vanessa and I don't take ourselves seriously. We love things that fool the eye, that have humor, that show a bit of eccentricity," Vreeland explains.

The villa's exterior definitely lives up to its two owners' whimsical, eclectic demands. There are Moghul-style cupolas, chimneys, and windows copied from the fa-

ABOVE: domes and chimneys on the roof were inspired by the 16th-century city of Fatephur Sikri in India. OPPOSITE: Marble and glass mosaics were ordered in Carrara and Murano for Villa Cafrevan's upper terrace swimming pool designed by Vanessa Somers.

RIGHT: different colors of adobe were used on a new tumbled-down, crosshatched wall made to look old. "We like anything that fools the eye," Vreeland says. OPPOSITE: grillwork covers Moghul-style windows. Heavy outside canvas curtains with black leather trim are copies of an ancient Roman design. Flanked by 16th-century Spanish columns is a *coin de repas*, or eating alcove; a 19th-century Kashmiri shawl covers the table. The villa's eclectic architecture includes a Moroccan brick arch, which frames a nearby palm tree.

bled city of Fatehpur Sikri in India; purposely half-ruined adobe walls with white checkerboard design are reminiscent of Moroccan kasbahs; heavy white canvas caidal-style curtains hang in doorways.

A protégé of Professor Odoardo Anselmi, head of the Vatican School of Mosaics, Somers designed the villa's swimming pool and personally laid thousands of Murano glass and Carrara marble mosaics at the bottom. Shimmering beneath the surface is an Italo-Moroccan landscape reminiscent of the work of Claude Lorrain.

ABOVE: colorful scraps of fabric decorate straw mats. RIGHT: striped canvas chairs, off-white umbrellas, and Berber straw mats are spread around the swimming pool each morning and returned to the pool room each evening.

A Former Harem

The unpretentious front door of American designer Bill Willis's house in the labyrinthine medina of Marrakesh faces onto a narrow alley. The Arabic writing spells his name.

AN AMERICAN FROM MISSISSIPPI, DESIGNER BILL WILLIS MOVED TO Morocco from Europe, where he worked in the 1960s. Among the first foreigners to settle deep in the Marrakesh medina, Willis bought and restored Dar Noujoun, House of the Stars, on the Rue Sebaatourigel. The harem of a royal palace, it is next to an Arab cemetery where the stern warning *Interdit Aux Non Muslemans* ("Forbidden to Non-Moslems") is painted forbiddingly on a crumbling wall. Known for his skill in adapting traditional high-style Hispano-Moorish architecture to Western tastes, the multitalented expatriate triggered a revival. Over the last twenty years, he has designed new and restored old properties throughout Marrakesh for a roster of clients that includes the Paul Gettys, Alain Delon, Yves Saint Laurent and Pierre Berge, and Marie-Hélène de Rothschild. He

A narrow staircase
containing a bronze
table and Berber
pot leads from the ground-
floor entrance hall
up to the reception rooms
on the second floor. For
parties, the staircase
is scattered with
rose petals.

also serves as design consultant to members of the royal family of Morocco.

Entered through a nondescript alley and up an inside stair with risers of glazed blue, black, and yellow tiles, Willis's own retreat is well known to hundreds of visitors to Morocco. Round-the-clock invitations to lunch, dinner, or cocktails allow friends and friends of friends to see one of the

ABOVE LEFT: an arrangement of roses fills a ceramic pot on a Moroccan rug. ABOVE: a 1st-century Roman bronze foot, a 17th-century Malasian *kreiss*, or dagger, and a 17th-century English embroidered box join forces on a 19th-century inlaid Moroccan table. LEFT: in Willis's old rose-colored living room, Renaissance bronze fire dogs add drama to his *tadelakt* and tile fireplace.

most superb restorations of a residence in Morocco.

First-time viewers are immediately struck by the house's fanciful Moroccan tile fireplaces and shiny *tadelakt* walls, both Willis trademarks. Originally used in *hammams*, or baths, *tadelakt* is a Moroccan wall treatment that combines plaster, sand, and natural coloring, polished to a high sheen with smooth stones and hand soap.

Tadelakt walls in oxblood, rust, gray, tan, and yellow are especially popular in Marrakesh. But

OPPOSITE: a long, narrow corridor with brick and *tadelakt* walls and floors of Moroccan tiles leads to the dining room and kitchen. LEFT: Willis often serves tea in his library. The mantel above his *tadelakt* and brick fireplace holds two 18th-century Moroccan vases and a 16th-century Turkish mortar.

RIGHT: a Moroccan-style *faux marbre* lantern sits on top of 19th-century Chinese fabric. BELOW: walls of exposed brick and tricolor *tadelakt* lend dramatic dimension to a fluted chimney in the dining room. An open-work opium table sits in an alcove behind an Afghan curtain; the embroidery on the pillow was commissioned and made in Marrakesh.

A maze of rooms and
hallways, the house
contains museum-
quality 18th- and 19th-
century painted wooden
doors and carved
wooden panels.
Moucharaby, traditional
turned wood in a mesh
design, can serve to
filter the harsh,
hot sunlight.

153

Willis's acclaimed courage with color extends to the aubergine, turquoise, mustard, crimson, navy blue, and green trim that outlines several doors along an entrance hall. The hall leads to a living room lit by candles at night, scented with sandalwood, and filled with Moroccan and European antiques. "When I first saw the room, which is twenty by twenty foot, I was amazed to realize it was square, not long and narrow like most Moroccan rooms. It was enough to make me buy the house," Willis recalls.

In the dining room, exposed layers of very thin bricks are alternate shades of mustard, burgundy, and beige. A dining table at Western height reveals Willis's refusal to sit cross-legged on the floor Moroccan-style. "I did it for years, but I'm back to my old American ways," he admits. "Tradition is fine, but it is comfort that counts."

In the master bedroom, an Iranian kilim hangs over a bed covered with a Bukhara embroidered spread and a Moroccan embroidered pillow. A pair of 1925 armchairs upholstered with contemporary Afghan kilims flanks a table covered with an Afghan tablecloth.

Tishka Hotel

The walls in the Moroccan dining room are *tadelakt,* a combination of sand and quicklime polished to look like Italian stucco.

UNLIKE MANY NATIONS, MOROCCO HAS KEPT ALIVE ITS centuries-old arts and crafts. In fact, the country's current craft renaissance began under King Hassan II, who reigned from 1961 to 1999, and who promoted a worldwide focus on Moroccan design. ✋ A visit to the much-lauded Tishka Hotel, designed by Tunis-born architect Charles Boccara and opened in 1986, reveals some of the finest examples of Moroccan artistic skills. ✋ The interior is designed by American Bill Willis who lives in Marrakesh, and whose clients are located around the globe. Ceiling and wall decoration, furniture, fireplaces, hardware, dinnerware, light fixtures, lanterns, fabrics—everything in the Tishka's public rooms and guest rooms has come from the multi-talented and widely acclaimed designer, who also skillfully directed their manufacture in Morocco.

ABOVE: A carved wooden railing resembles *moucharaby*, panels used to cover harem windows.
BELOW: Fanciful columns in the dining room provide the effect of a palm oasis. RIGHT: A Moroccan lantern hangs from the four-story main salon.
FAR RIGHT: Panels of High Atlas hilltowns are by Christian Granville.

"Quality handicraft, pride and intuitive understanding of precedents still go together in Morocco," Willis says in his soft Mississippi drawl. "This country is exceptional. Moroccans are some of the finest, affordable artisans to be found anywhere in the world."

Known for his ability to create a livable modern-day property with historic Moroccan features, Willis has a remarkable sense of color. From its turquoise-trimmed exterior windows to the egg-yolk interior walls, Tishka Hotel boasts a color palette inspired by Berber rugs and textiles.

The Souk

"BALEK, BALEK!" "MAKE WAY, MAKE WAY!" 🖐 CRIES ARE HEARD as mule trains weave through souks, or markets, in every small village and large town in Morocco. They are all things to all people. A labyrinth of small shops, a souk is boutique, flea market, recycling center, supermarket, department store, open-air reception with receiving line, circus, sideshow, and mob scene all at the same time. 🖐 Shaded by loose reed mat "ceilings" that slash the air with dusty shadows and bright bars of scorching sunlight, the serpentine alleys and dead ends of a souk are lined with shops, each with its own specialty: rugs, copperware, furniture, kitchenware, silk tassels, herbal medicines, slippers, and antique windows and doors. 🖐 Burlap bags overflow with cardamom, cumin, and coriander. There are mounds of mint, pickled olives, and dates. Wooden crates spill over

ABOVE: for centuries, donkeys have carried merchandise in and out of the narrow lanes in souks. RIGHT: Berber jewelry and a *jebana* await sale in the souk in Taroudant. OPPOSITE: even chickens are available in the souk.

with citrus. Fresh loaves of bread are stacked up like poker chips. Clothing racks dip low from the weight of men's *djellabas* and *burnooses* and women's caftans.

The souk in Fez is the oldest, most medieval, most replete with traditional Moroccan handicrafts. With the largest selection of fine rugs, antique Berber jewelry, and pots from the Sahara, the souk in Marrakesh is the most frenzied and most touristy.

The Marrakesh souk also offers a good deal more than shopping. Here each evening, entertainers turn the Place Djemaa El Fna into one of the greatest shows on earth. Sorcerers, comedians, story-tellers, wrestlers, boxers, snake charmers, and acrobats join forces to produce a ten-ring circus, one that has been going on daily for centuries. "In the beginning," it is said, "there was the Djemaa El Fna."

RIGHT: Shop signs such as this gigantic flounder outside a seafood store are common. The hand of Fatima averts the evil eye. **OVERLEAF:** Moroccan women shop daily in the thousands of souks for everything from food to cosmetics. Newsprint often serves as wrapping, and in the country, there are even "parking lots" for donkeys. Vendors expect that bargaining will play a part in each transaction, whether it be for a woven basket or the dried rose petals displayed in a basket.

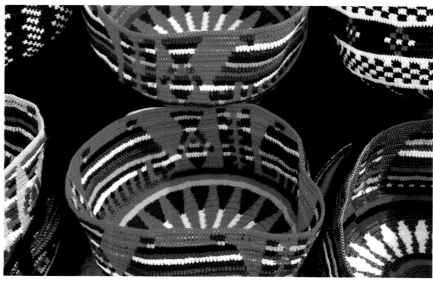

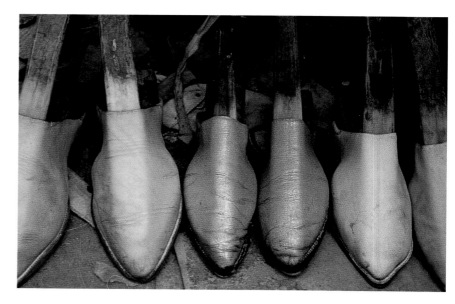

OPPOSITE: donkey saddles, woven bread baskets, pottery, and Berber jewelry: contemporary folk art as well as antique handicrafts are for sale in a souk. LEFT: deep-fried doughnuts are strung on a grass reed for a hungry buyer.

169

ABOVE: woven Berber bread
baskets from around
Marrakesh await export
from the souk to New
Mexico. RIGHT: men gossip
and haggle over prices in
the souk in Tafrout.

Decorative Arts

A painter completes work on a ceiling panel commissioned in his workshop in the Fez souk. When it is finished, it will be taken to the house and installed.

THE FIRST-TIME VISITOR TO MOROCCO MAY BE DAZZLED BY THE colorful and courageous combinations of tiles, plasterwork, and painted surfaces on walls, doors, shutters, ceilings, and floors in private houses and hotels as well as in the arches and on pathways leading into buildings. But Moroccans have traditionally relied on the decoration of walls, ceilings, and floors to "furnish" a house. A proverb explains why Moroccans have always made the courtyards, reception rooms, and living areas of their homes rich in ornate details. They are adherents of the belief that "the first thing one should own is a home; and it is the last thing one should sell, for a home is one's tomb this side of heaven." This combines with the belief of Abu 'Inan, a 14th-century homeowner: "That which is beautiful is not dear at any cost, and that which pleases man cannot be too expensive."

173

Painted Surfaces

MOROCCANS ARE MASTERS OF painted wood and gypsum, or plaster of Paris, surfaces. Following the Prophet's command not to depict humans, they paint trees, elaborate and stylized flower bouquets, ingeniously varied motifs of sinuous vines, leaf-shaped arabesques, and inanimate objects. Ornate, colorful, abstract Islamic designs with strong mathematical symmetry are rendered by artists who seek to transport viewers into a state of uplifted thought.

Berber painters too are adept at painting on wood. Rich in symbolism and conveying ancient mystical messages, Berber painted surfaces are abstract; and because Berbers are less likely to adhere to the strictures of Islamic design, their painted surfaces are a great deal more personal and often

ABOVE LEFT: calligraphy in bright colors decorates the exteriors of buildings in Asilah, a fishing village on the Atlantic seacoast. LEFT: elaborate repeated motifs are worked in paint on gypsum. OPPOSITE: Mustapha Boumazzourh, a sculptor, designed and painted a contemporary Moroccan motif on a door at his 19th-century Essaouira farmhouse.

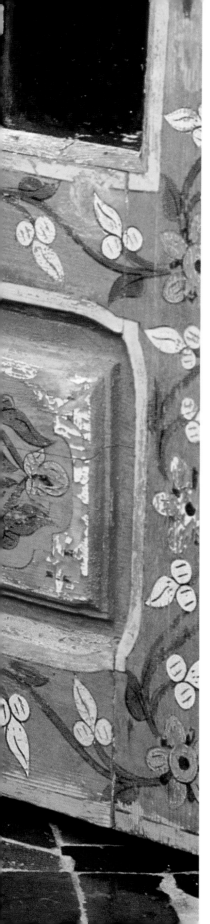

combine unexpected colors.

Firm believers that a wooden piece is not finished until it is covered with decorations, Moroccan homeowners and designers keep the country's *zawwaga*, or painters on wood, in heavy demand. Each job is different. Like their ancestors, Moroccan *zawwaga* today spend weeks, even months, working on wooden cupolas, alcoves, doors, and ceilings in pri-

vate houses and new hotels.

Like all skilled craftsmen and artisans in Morocco, painters work under a *maallem*, or master craftsman. Some stand up while painting; others sit cross-legged. They hold their brushes, which are made out of hair from donkey tails, vertically, their wrists supported by their left hands to allow fingers to be completely supple.

Colors are applied first; the out-

OPPOSITE: a painted door to the restaurant Yacout in Marrakesh opens onto a corridor laid with brick-shaped tiles from Fez. ABOVE: many painters decorate town walls and doors along the narrow streets of Asilah during the annual summer arts festival.

177

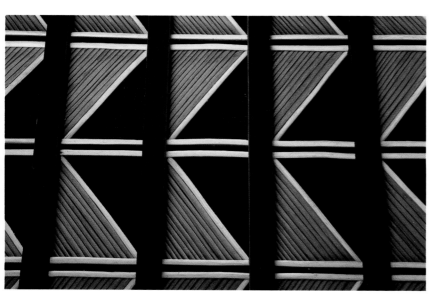

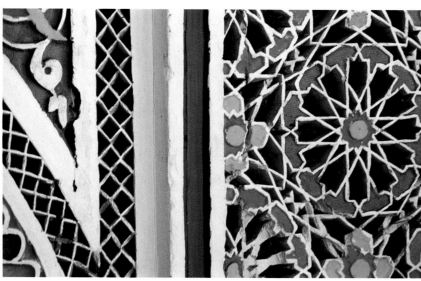

lines that emphasize contours come later. To the distress of purists, the natural, vibrant egg-yolk-based colors of the past reminiscent of the brilliance seen in medieval manuscripts have given way to the strident colors of modern-day chemical paints.

Workers in gypsum or plaster of Paris are equally respected in Morocco for their technical and artistic skills. After a specialist has drawn endlessly repeated motifs of squares, circles, triangles, stylized stars, almonds, flowers, even scallop shells, plasterwork artists, or *ghabbar*, carve reliefs in four or five layers, both on the surface of a wall and in hollowed-out details that vary in depth.

Plaster of Paris in Morocco is either left its natural eggshell color or polychromed in vibrant primary colors.

RIGHT: this handpainted late 19th-century door is one of many surrounding the garden courtyard at the Museum of Moroccan Arts in Rabat. BELOW RIGHT: the Mediterranean villa of Madame Sete Guetta in Cabo Negro contains superb examples of early 19th-century painted furniture from nearby Tetouan. OPPOSITE: a 19th-century Berber ceiling from the Bert Flint collection in Marrakesh. Berber houses are decorated with warm colors and geometric designs, both whimsical and symbolic.

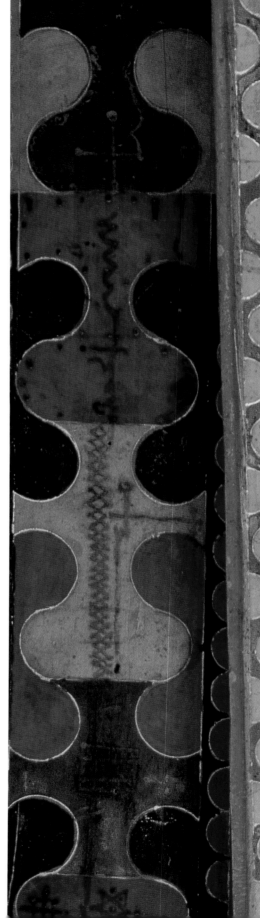

180

Ghabbar, or master artisans of gypsum, carve decorative reliefs that may be left a natural eggshell color or polychromed in rich vibrant hues. The scallop wall panel at left is from the sultan's palace in Tangier.

Tiles

DECORATIVE AS WELL AS STRUC-
tural and architectural, Moroccan
handmade tiles are among the
most colorful in the world. De-
rived from Byzantine and Roman
mosaics, *zelliges*, or wall tiles, are
Morocco's great specialty, both in
the skill with which they are made
and because of the expertise with
which they are laid. Traditionally,
they have been used for inside
decoration in wall panels, staircases, archways, and columns.
Today, foreign designers order
zelliges to be made in their own
colors and shapes and use them in
tables, fireplaces, picture frames,
even chairs.

Moroccan tile production has
long been centered in Fez. Adher-
ing to the centuries-old process,
local clay is thrown into basins
carved in the ground and is then

**French architect Michel
Pinseau has designed
the Hassan II mosque in
Casablanca. Many
interior walls are
covered with Moroccan
tiles exhibiting a modern
approach to traditional
Islamic design. The
pentacle and crescent
moon, the national
emblem of Morocco, is
the central motif in
this tile panel.**

Wall tiles in the Saadian
tombs, built in
Marrakesh by Ahmed
Edh Dhahabi at the end
of the 16th century,
are elaborately patterned.

mixed with water. After a twenty-four-hour stabilizing period, an *ajjan*, or mixer, kneads the clay. He eliminates any stones, bits of wood, or other foreign elements. Next, a *fakhkhar*, or workman, molds the clay into rectangular slabs that are dried in the sun, coated with different colored glazes, and fired. The ovens are heated with wood, grasses, and crushed olive pits, and the temperature inside will reach eight hundred degrees.

The unique aspect of making *zelliges* begins next. A designer traces the outline of the pieces to be cut out of the tile slab. He makes his design with an *ud el khizran*, or bamboo stick, dipped in ink. Andre Paccard displays more than 350 different shapes and sizes in his book *Traditional Islamic Craft in Moroccan Architecture.* Some are so small, 150 can fit on a matchbook cover.

ABOVE LEFT: designer Bill Willis sought to update and give new direction to traditional Islamic design in the tile fireplaces and furnishings of the Tishka Hotel in Marrakesh. LEFT: with bases of plaster of Paris, columns in the courtyard of the Palais Mokri in Fez are covered with traditional *zelliges,* or tiles. The stained glass in the window was imported from Italy.

The final and most delicate step is the actual cutting out of the *zelliges* from the slab. This is the work of a *taksir*, or tile cutter, who uses a hammer that has been sharpened on both sides. Filed smooth and sorted according to shape, size, and color, the *zelliges* are then taken to the job site and laid into patterns by a *maallem*.

Traditional patterns, with such evocative names as hen's feet, divided tears, little tambourine, and heifer's eyes, are most common. But contemporary adaptations of traditional Islamic designs are beginning to be introduced. Regardless, the patterns must always conform to the Islamic geometric grid. The result is that Moroccan tile designs cannot be judged by the originality of the design but by the combinations of colors and the flair with which the *maallem* has depicted crescents, triangles, stars, lozenges, and squares.

LEFT: detail of tiles designed by Bill Willis for his fireplace in Marrakesh. The *ferragha,* or layer of tiles, has performed his task with painstaking skill.
ABOVE: garden paths in the 17th-century palace built by Moulay Ismael in Tangier are of brick with accent tiles.
OVERLEAF: traditional Islamic designs are not judged by the originality of their designs but by the combinations of colors. Innovative tiles in the Hassan II mosque in Casablanca point away from the ages-old traditional Islamic patterns.

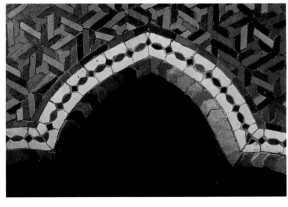  

A Contemporary Renovation

With deft window treatments, American designer Stewart Church turned a nondescript modern house near Tangier into a dramatic neo-Islamic weekend retreat for Mina and Salah Balafrej.

MOROCCANS AND FOREIGNERS ALIKE ARE REDISCOVERING TANGIER'S centuries-old international appeal. Ideally located for weekend excursions across the Mediterranean to nearby Spain, the city offers a unique Moroccan–European life-style. Former king, Hassan II renovated a palace in Tangier. So too has a princess from the Middle East. ✋ Add to the list Mina and Salah Balafrej from Rabat. Expatriate American designer Stewart Church helped the couple reinterpret an existing modern house on Sharf Hill, overlooking the harbor. With Church's renovation, it has become one of Morocco's most dramatic contemporary private residences. Of special significance are the houses' windows, doors, and latticework. Here it is clear that contemporary homeowners are beginning to embellish their houses' exteriors. Knowing that Moroccans in the 19th century were fond of

bright colors, Church convinced the Balafrejs to look back in time and be equally bold. The house's formal Moroccan reception room with its striking red *tadelakt* walls is a tour de force of neo-Islamic design.

Other rooms contain Moroccan and European furniture arrangements—new and old—which combine to make the Balafrej house one of the most fresh and sophisticated mixes of traditional Moroccan and Western design in the country.

LEFT: a large glass-top table for serving food at parties reflects the striking red *tadelakt* interior of the reception room. Handpainted doors were designed by Church and made in the souk. ABOVE: especially noteworthy is the latticework Church designed for the facades.

A mezzanine sitting room opens onto a dining room, with views of the Mediterranean.

196

ABOVE: Moorish-style architectural symmetry dramatizes the flow of space. FAR LEFT: a sitting room includes European sofas and Moroccan-inspired torchères, tables, and chairs designed by Church. LEFT: detail of painted dome in living room.

A Bit of Old England

Pink exterior walls and turquoise shutters give the wisteria-covered house of David Herbert in Tangier a southern Mediterranean feeling reminiscent of Provence. The Haitian watercolor was bought at the local flea market.

IN THE LATE 1940S, DAVID HERBERT, SON OF THE FIFTEENTH EARL of Pembroke, moved permanently from Wilton, his ancestral home in England, to Tangier. ✋ The doyen of the city's international foreign colony, he remembers the 1950s and 1960s, when Tangier was a mecca for hedonists anxious to experience the go-for-broke pleasures of North Africa; and he appreciates that times have changed. Tangier is now a quiet haven for cosmopolites grateful to live comfortably and privately—in Morocco yet within sight of Europe. ✋ Caroubia, Herbert's rambling two-story Provençal-style pink house—with shutters painted a startling Matisse turquoise—was the retreat of the 19th-century mystic Sidi Amar. It is set in La Montaigne, a popular residential area where the king and several foreign princes and princesses have palaces. ✋ One passes through arched Moroccan door-

OPPOSITE: the wall surrounding the heavy wooden front door is inset with sea shells; a 17th-century William Kent mirror and 19th-century French prints decorate the foyer. Out back, a pair of contemporary Italian ceramic guard dogs flanks a terrace leading to Herbert's vast, semitropical garden. A French wrought-iron chair in the shape of a swan lends a note of whimsy and charm to the garden. RIGHT: full of 18th- and 19th-century English, French, and Italian furniture and paintings, the European-style drawing rooms in Caroubia are entered through Moroccan-style doorways. Vases of fresh flowers compete for space on tables crowded with photographs of well-known friends—the Queen Mother, Barbara Hutton, and Cecil Beaton among them.

ways into what is otherwise a very European household. Like other Tangier houses owned by European expatriates who surrounded themselves with the familiar, Caroubia makes few concessions to its Moroccan location. Indeed, Herbert's cozy, chintz-filled rooms are full of mainly English furniture as well as paintings by Van Dyck, Reynolds, Augustus John, Cecil Beaton, Claudio Bravo, and Rex Whistler.

The 18th- and 19th-century English chairs, sofas, bureaus, picture and mirror frames are gilded, lacquered, and often carved. "Directoire, regency, rococo, and chinoiserie—I love them all. It's hard to choose," says Herbert. The surprise is the palette. Walls of egg-yolk yellow, lime green, and Rajastan pink all testify to Herbert's exuberant style. "White is so boring," he confides.

The lime colored walls of the main salon are hung with paintings brought by Herbert from Wilton, his ancestral home. Van Dyck's "Countess of Pembroke" hangs over the fireplace between a pair of 18th-century Italian mirrors; across the room is a self-portrait by Sir Thomas Lawrence.

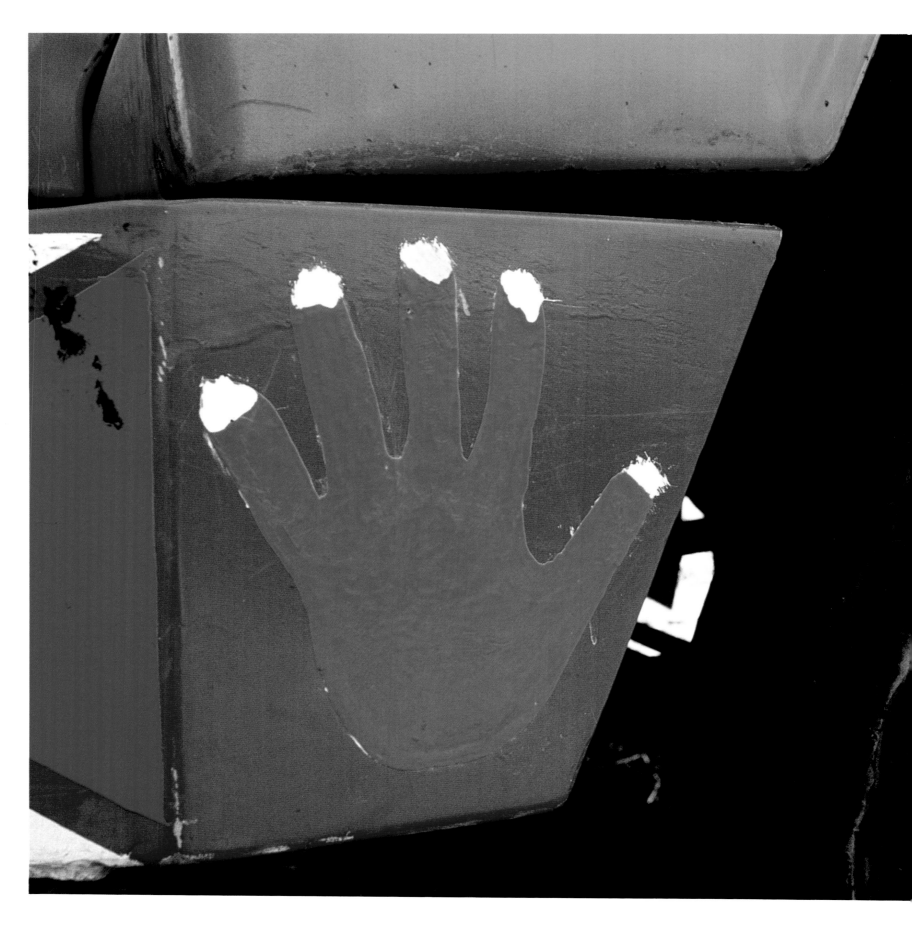

Color

BENEATH MOROCCO'S CLOUDLESS BLUE SKIES ARE BONE-WHITE towns and multicolored fishing ports. The same landscape can be a tapestry of bright wildflowers in spring and a monotonous carpet of stubble in summer. Stalls in the souks spill over with multihued fruits and vegetables. Woven baskets mix colors that clash brilliantly. Tiles offer a kaleidoscope of color. ✋ Tradition-steeped artisans in Morocco continue to demonstrate an innate color sense as compelling today as it was to Matisse in the early 20th century. Palace throne rooms, Berber houses in the Atlas, bolts of cloth in Chaouen, sugar cones wrapped in paper, women's veils and caftans, men's leather slippers—there is color everywhere in Morocco. It is in tiles, in fabrics, and on walls, shutters, and doors. Subtle and soft, bold and bright, color is part of Morocco's magic.

A primary blue hand of Fatima stands in sharp relief against the hot pink of a truck's splash guard.

OPPOSITE: a dappled veil shields the face of a woman in Taroudant. LEFT: a rich red banner incorporating the Moroccan star is draped across a palm-frond fence.

LEFT: the stark white that is such a signature of the walls and doorways of Chaouen is created by white lye. **OPPOSITE:** banners of many colors are hung beneath the reed roofs that cover the aisles of many souks.

OPPOSITE: at a café in Rabat, tables and chairs are painted blue; the color is believed to ward off evil spirits. LEFT: the walls of a courtyard in Asilah are painted lime and off-white; black is a traditional color for men's *burnooses*.

Modern calligraphic
tiles at the Hassan II mosque are
in a rich panoply of colors.

La Mamounia

CERTAIN LANDMARK BUILDINGS IN THE WORLD DO NOT NEED street addresses; everyone knows where and what they are. La Mamounia is one of them. Say the name and travelers' eyes instantly light up. They know it is a hotel in Marrakesh, an acclaimed hotel with an astonishing history, a Moorish-style hotel with Art Deco features, a hotel with phenomenal gardens. ✋ For those fortunate enough to check into La Mamounia, it is a step back into Moroccan history. The story begins in the 18th century when an extraordinary park outside the kasbah in Marrakesh—one of Morocco's four Imperial Cities—was given as a wedding present to Prince Moulay Mamoun by his parents Sultan Sidi Muhammad and Lalla Fatima. Named after the prince, *Arset el Mamoun* was famous for its beauty and for the frequent festivities that were held there to entertain royal guests.

ABOVE: On warm days, doormen at La Mamounia wear all white; on cool days, they switch to black burnooses. RIGHT: The many indoor fountains are filled daily with roses from the hotel's gardens, a favorite painting location of Winston Churchill.

It became clear in the 1920s that Marrakesh needed a glamorous hotel to host European travelers. The park was the obvious site. Under the direction of European architects, La Mamounia was built by French, Italian and Moroccan craftsmen to showcase the finest Moroccan and Art Deco design and furniture. Its doors opened in 1923, and guests have included film stars, royalty and heads of state.

Regularly renovated over the last half-century, La Mamounia has mercifully maintained its historic integrity. Burled wood and marquetry panels appear throughout the dimly lit lobby. Stepping from the hotel's mirrored dark-wood and glass elevators, guests open doors to rooms that are reminiscent of a pasha's palace.

A night in the Churchill Suite evokes a more Anglo-Saxon atmosphere. In homage to Sir Winston, who was a frequent

guest, an easel displays a replica of one of his many paintings of the hotel's famous gardens.

Sprawled across 20 acres, cared for by 34 full-time gardeners and designed in formal Moroccan style, La Mamounia's semitropical gardens intoxicate strollers with blossoming orange and lemon trees, thousands of rose bushes, and masses of bright mimosa. Nightingales and turtledoves nest in the palm trees that line the pathways between herbaceous

LEFT: A waiter in La Mamounia's Moroccan restaurant stands guard over a plate of *b'stilla*, a *millefeuille* of pigeon, almonds, spices, and chopped hard-boiled eggs. **ABOVE:** Enormous flowerbeds that line the gardens' pathways are full of snapdragons, pansies and other colorful flowers.

gardens planted with stock, snap-dragons, and hollyhocks. Over the top of the bougainvillea-covered walls, the distant, snowcapped mountains of the High Atlas provide an impressive backdrop to this North African Shangri-la.

ABOVE: Tilework, rugs, bedspreads: some guest rooms at La Mamounia are decorated in typical Moroccan style. RIGHT: Throughout the hotel, huge glazed water jars remind visitors of North Africa's arid climate.

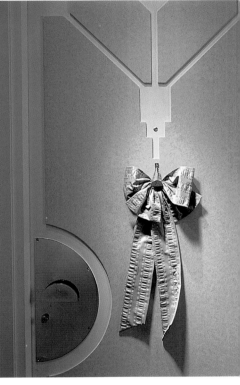

LEFT: Bartering is often integral to the experience of shopping in Marrakesh's souk, but contemporary jewelers set fixed prices for reworked antique jewelry. ABOVE: A green bow on a door means, "Please make up this guest room."

A Berber-Style Farmhouse

FORERUNNERS OF THE CURRENT INTERNATIONAL BUILDING BOOM IN the Palmeraie outside Marrakesh, the Bernard Levys were pioneers. Residents of Casablanca and Paris, the Moroccan-born couple built a vacation "farmhouse" beneath the towering palm. A high adobe wall keeps the farmhouse from view, while a constant cacophony of braying donkeys, quacking ducks, crowing roosters, and gobbling turkeys helps to conceal the fact the house is only fifteen minutes from downtown. ✋ "We wanted the Marrakesh house to have an earthy, Berber quality," the couple says to explain the building's exterior. It is made from thin red bricks with beige mortar in between, a characteristic of villages in the southern Sahara. ✋ Nestled in a garden full of olive and citrus trees and surrounded by fields of wheat dappled with red poppies, the one-story house's outside windows are painted

ABOVE: striped silk pillows are stuffed into a Berber chest that has been painted inside and out. RIGHT: in the dining room, wood and leather stools surround the hand-painted table. OPPOSITE: embroidered curtains from Fez are used to conceal the sleeping alcove. The spread is a French lace tablecloth; the pillows are from the souk.

bright blue. Antique Moroccan doors inside the house reemphasize the Levys' insistence on historic local authenticity.

With herringbone floors of terra-cotta, burnt umber, and olive-colored baby bricks, the living room has coffee tables made from native thuya wood from Essaouira. Off-white muslin is used both for curtains and to cover modern sofas.

The "Berber country" look continues in an adjacent guesthouse. Entered through dazzling blue doors, bedrooms full of antique handpainted furniture are off an all-white courtyard the floor of which is covered with bright yellow-and-blue tiles.

"The house is exactly what we wanted. It is barefoot, Moroccan country," the Levys are happy to say. "The way we live in Marrakesh is a happy change from Casablanca and Paris."

OPPOSITE: muslin curtains and upholstery lend an air of coolness to the living room, with its white tray ceiling. The furniture is handmade and contemporary. ABOVE: an iodized metal jug sits in the garden outside a bedroom window.

ABOVE: a hand-painted cupboard is used for storing pottery in the kitchen. ABOVE RIGHT: a painted wood panel adds a further decorative element to the kitchen. RIGHT: chickens have nested outside the kichen door. FAR RIGHT: mattresses air in the tiled courtyard outside of the guest house.

A North African Paradise

The Majorelle Garden in Marrakesh was planted in the 1920s by French painter Jacques Majorelle. Parisian designer Yves Saint Laurent and his partner Pierre Bergé restored it in the 1960s.

THE VILLA OASIS. THE NAME IS PERFECT. RING THE BELL, WAIT in the hot sun for the elderly retainer to swing open the gate, step inside out of the sight and sound of honking traffic, chattering pedestrians, and yelling vendors. ✋ Instantly, the cacophony of teeming Marrakesh is gone, replaced by a serenity, a peace, and an astonishing beauty. You are inside the walls of the world-famous Moroccan hideaway of Paris couturier Yves Saint Laurent and his business partner Pierre Bergé. ✋ Born and brought up in Algiers, Saint Laurent's lifelong passion for Islamic culture burst into architectural and horticultural bloom when he and Bergé bought the former villa and garden of French artist Jacques Majorelle. ✋ Madly in love with Marrakesh and all things Moroccan, Majorelle arrived in the country in 1917 and remained until his death in 1962. Soon afterwards, Saint

ABOVE: The Villa Oasis, like many Moroccan residences, hides behind high walls. A courtyard pool reflects hundreds of species of flowers and trees, many from abroad. RIGHT: The vivid blue lends additional sensuality to the garden's exoticism.

Laurent and Bergé—with the help of Marrakesh designer Bill Willis and Parisian designer Jacques Granges—set about restoring the 1924 villa into a Marrakesh bolt hole of magnificent design, which includes Islamic-inspired pieces by Saint Laurent and Willis. Furniture, fabrics, paintings, rugs, ceilings, doorways—everything in the villa is statement to an arrestingly exotic taste set off by dazzling surroundings.

It is the adjacent Majorelle Garden, however, that most people exclaim over. Open to the public, it is a one-acre North African botanical paradise that has been restored and expanded by Saint Laurent with breathtaking daring.

The garden's bougainvillea-covered adobe walls, Moorish- and Art Deco–inspired buildings, and raised flowerbeds of nasturtiums are painted a strong hard blue, known as "bleu Majorelle." Large terracotta pots, painted pale yellow, green and blue and spilling over with flamingo-colored

LEFT: Working with designers Bill Willis in Marrakesh and Jacques Granges in Paris, Yves Saint Laurent turned his villa into a museum of Moroccan handicraft. ABOVE: Ceilings and doors reflect ancient Moorish designs.

LEFT AND TOP RIGHT: Few surfaces in the Villa Oasis remain unadorned. Walls and ceilings are frequently decorated with hand-painted tiles made in Fez and showing traditional Moroccan motifs. BELOW: Antique Berber beads embellish a 19th-century French bronze of a North African chieftain. BOTTOM RIGHT: Bathroom tiles are laid in a pattern designed by Bill Willis.

geraniums, are strategically placed along crisscrossing paths of beaten red earth and tile steps that are colored hot blue and chilli green. Carp and goldfish streak through pools full of water lilies and papyruses. Dappled sunlight comes and goes through the luxuriant swaying foliage of towering—and often rare—bamboo, palm trees, agaves, and cacti.

ABOVE: The living room of the Villa Oasis is formal. LEFT: The upstairs sitting room is more relaxed and open to the breezes. BELOW: The extraordinary plaster of Paris framework around a door exemplifies the high-quality Islamic detailing throughout the villa.

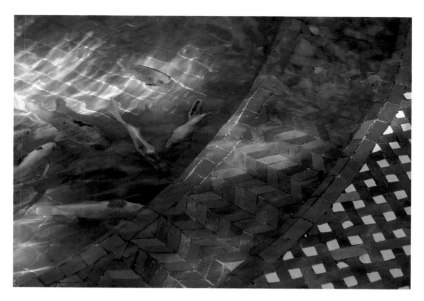

ABOVE: Fish in tiled pools, vermilion and fuchsia bougainvillea on trellises, red geraniums in blue pots: the hot color palette of the Majorelle Garden competes with Morocco's eye-catching Berber textiles and rugs. RIGHT: Garden buildings are painted bleu Majorelle, doors and window grills are in a citrus lemon.

Travel to Morocco

FOR THOSE FLYING FROM THE United States to Morocco, Royal Air Maroc is the only airline that flies directly from New York City. Flights leave New York in the early evening and arrive in Casablanca the following morning.

There are direct connecting flights from Casablanca for Tangier, Agadir, and Marrakesh.

Flights from Morocco to the United States depart the airport in Casablanca in the morning, arriving in New York in the afternoon the same day.

There are daily flights to and from all major European cities on Royal Air Maroc and other European carriers.

All major automobile rental agencies have offices at the Casablanca airport. Car rentals are expensive; therefore, a group traveling together to Morocco may wish to consider renting a car, or a van, with a driver. It may turn out to be less expensive.

The average length of stay in Morocco is seven to fifteen days. In that time, a great deal can be seen. Distances between interesting towns and cities are not large, and traveling them rarely takes more than a half day or a full day. The roads are good. And the scenery and stopoff points are beautiful and interesting.

Ramadan, a religious festival that vaguely parallels the Christian Lent, occurs in the spring. It is observed by all faithful Moroccans, who may neither drink nor eat from dawn until dusk. During Ramadan many restaurants and shops are closed during the day. However, they are open at night, and hotel restaurants remain open for guests and tourists.

French is spoken throughout Morocco, together with Arabic and Berber. English is spoken by hotel and restaurant staffs almost everywhere.

In Morocco, unlike other Moslem countries, outsiders are not permitted to enter mosques.

Female visitors to Morocco will feel more comfortable in blouses, skirts, and pants—rather than shorts—when exploring the cities and towns.

Shoppers' Guide

THE FOLLOWING IS IN NO WAY A list of "recommended" shops and craftsmen, but it is a place to get started both in Morocco and the rest of the world. Moroccan cities are full of stores selling Moroccan crafts, and their souks are full of talented craftsmen. One must go, see, decide for oneself. In the last few years, a number of shops and stores in Great Britain and the United States have developed their ethnic arts-and-crafts ranges, and a few focus exclusively on Morocco. There is no question, it is easier to deal with a "home base" outlet than it is to search out, bargain over, and go through the hassle of shipping something from Morocco. But shopping in Morocco is great fun, although you must keep the rules of the game very much in mind.

It is often difficult for the novice to tell the difference between yesterday's treasure and today's reproduction, especially when the seller insists that everything over fifty years old is "antique." The system demands comparative shopping before bargaining down the price for *anything and everything* for a good deal less than originally asked. Because bargaining is expected in Morocco, store owners expect to settle on a price anywhere from 25 to 50 percent less than originally asked, both in and out of the souks.

When shopping in Morocco, one must be alert to the fact that if a guide takes you to a store, or your hotel recommends a store, the chances are high that the prices will be as much as 50 percent over what the store owner would have started bargaining at if you had gone there alone. Because "those who help" will get a cut of the deal, to shop on your own is to save a great deal of money.

Morocco

CASABLANCA

Art de Fez
Rue General Laperine, No. 6

FEZ

Au Petit Bazar de Bon Accueil
35 Talaa Sghira
Medina Ancienne

Boutique Majid
Abdelmajid Rais El Fenni
66 Rue des Chretiens

MARRAKESH

Adolfo de Velasco
La Mamounia

Al Yed Gallery
66 Fhal Chidmi
Rue Mouassine

L'Art de Goulimine
25 Souk des Tapis

L'Art Marocain
50 Kzadriya Bab Mellah

Atika Boutique
34 Rue de la Liberté

Bab Chem's
24 Quartier Industriel Sidi Ghanem Route de Safi

Bazar du Sud
117 Souk des Tapis

Chez Alaoui
Souk Shouari
Ghassoul No. 42

Chez Les Brodeuses Arabes
12 Rue Rahba Lakdima

Chez Moulay
Rue Rahba El Biadyne No. 42

Clayna Bazaar
El Kadima No. 73
Le Coffret de Santal
La Mamounia

Coopartim
Ensemble Artisanal
Avenue Mohammed V

Dar El Kasbah
41 Rue de la Radeema

Fondouk El Fatmi
Bab Ftouh

Fondouk El Quarzaza Bn 24
56 Place Bab Ftouh

La Lampe d'Aladin
99 and 70 bis Rue Semmarine

Mamounia Arts
47 Rue Dar El Bacha
Bab Doukkala

Moroccan Arts
67 Sabeb Mouley Hadj
El Kssour

L'Oiseau Bleu
3 Rue Tarik Ibn Ziad

L'Orientaliste
15 Rue de la Liberté

La Porte d'Or
II5 Souk Semmarine

R/Bati
41 Rue Dar el Bacha

Reminiscence
Sourya No. 7

Rhalid Art Gallery
14 Rue Dar el Bacha

Siwa
124 Rue Dar el Bacha

Touflight Boutique
7 Souk El Fakharin

RABAT

Gallerie Cheremetieff
16 bis Rue Aannaba

SAFI

Serghini Ahmed
7 Souk des Poteries

TANGIER

Adolfo de Velasco
28 Blvd. Mohammed V

Arditti
87 Rue de la Liberté

Bazar Sebou
18 Rue Sebou

Boutique Majid
66 Rue des Chretiens

United States
(Country code: 1)

La Boheme
222 W. Colorado
Telluride, CO 81435
Tel: 970.728.1233

Brooke Pickering
Moroccan Rugs
1209 Rt. 213, P.O. Box 37
High Falls, NY 12440
Tel: 845.687.8737

Circa
405 North Guadalupe
Santa Fe
NM 87501
Tel: 505.989.9001

Cobwebs
116 West Houston St.
New York, NY10012
Tel: 212.505.1558

Eye of the Ra
533I Southwest Macadam
Portland, OR 97201
Tel: 503.224.4292

Eziba
87 Marshall St.
Bldg. 1 at Mass. MOCA
No. Adams, MA 01247
Tel: 413.664.9999

Maxim Designs
4633 Wornall Rd.
Kansas City, MO 64112
Tel: 816.753.7399

Native Creations
26881 Avenida Los Palmas, Suite B
Dana Point, CA 92624
Tel: 949.493.7077

Nomad
2407 18th St., N.W.
Washington, DC 20009
Tel: 202.332.2998

Nomad
279 Newbury St.
Boston, MA 02116
Tel: 617.297.9677

Nomads
207 Shelby St.
Santa Fe, NM 87501
Tel: 505.986.0855

Gary Owens
6II6 No. Central, Suite 200
Dallas, TX 75206
Tel: 214.526.2290

Phoenix
Highway 1
Big Sur, CA 93920
Tel: 408.667.2347

Sam's Souk
979 Lexington Avenue
New York, New York 10021
Tel: 212.5325.7210

Sam's Souk Two, Inc.
321 1/2 Bleeker St.
New York, NY 10014
Tel: 212.691.0726

Showcase at the Peak
23425 N. Scottsdale
Scottsdale, AZ 85255
Tel: 602.585.0005

Le Souk
1001 East Alameda
Santa Fe, MN 87501
Tel: 505.989.8765

Surroundings
1710 Sunset Blvd.
Houston, TX 77005
Tel: 713.527.9838

Third World
358-3 World Trade Center
P.O. Box 581075
Dallas, TX 75258
Tel: 214.741.3583

Tierra del Lagarto 7812 East Acoma
Suite 8
Scottsdale, AZ 85250
Tel: 480.609.1289

Topnotch
Walnut Ave. Mall
620 Sun Valley Rd.
Ketchum, ID 83340
Tel: 208.726.7797

Uriah Heep's
303 E. Hopkins
Aspen, CO 81611
Tel: 303.925.7456

Great Britain
(Country code: 44)

Chandni Chowk
1 Harlequins
Paul Street
Exeter
Devon, EX4 3TT
Tel: 01392 410201
(Rugs, pottery)

Graham & Green
4 Elgin Crescent
London W11
Tel: 020 7727 4594
(Lamps, pottery, wooden articles)

Joss Graham Oriental Textiles
10 Eccleston Street
London SW1 9LT
Tel: 020 7730 4370

The Kilim House
28A Pickets Street
London SW12 8QB
Tel: 020 8675 3122

Liberty plc
210/220 Regent Street
London W1R 6AH
Tel: 020 7734 1234
(Pottery, mirrors, fabric)

Moroccan Rugs and Weavings
5A Calabria Road
London N5 1JB
Tel: 020 7226 7908
(Rugs)

Nice Irma's
Unit 2, Finchley Industrial Centre
879 High Road
London N12 8QA
Tel: 020 8343 9766
(Pottery, jewelry, mirrors)

On Show
19 Short's Gardens
Covent Garden
London WC2H 9AT
Tel: 020 7240 9731
(Pottery)

Verandah
15B Blenheim Crescent
London W11 2EE
Tel: 020 7792 9289
(Pottery and lanterns)

Antiques

OLD POTTERY; EMBROIDERY; FUR-
niture; jewelry; rugs; handcarved and
painted wood doors, windows, and
chests; wrought-iron grillwork to
cover windows: they can all be found
in every Moroccan city and town, in
souks, in shops, at street markets.
Moroccans and visitors alike join
ranks to discover and bargain over
the country's occasionally old, and
very often made-to-look-old arts
and crafts. When buying anything
"antique" at what can be a high
price, *caveat emptor* must be kept
uppermost in mind.

Wood

THUYA WOOD IS SIMILAR TO BURLED
walnut in appearance. Varying in
shades from dark mahogany to
sprightly pear or cherry, thuya grows
in the forests around Essaouira.
Thousands of woodcarvers sit daily
making boxes, chess sets, frames,
obelisks, and bookends, most of
which are exported to Europe, where
prices are often 500 percent higher
than in Essaouira.

CASABLANCA

Az-El-Arab Benlamlih
24 Bis Rue de Briey
Bd. Mustapha El Maani

Centre de Formation Professionnelle
327 Blvd. 2 Mars

Chraibi Mohamed
6 Rue General Laparine

Slimani Mohamed
Lot. Laayoune No. 31
Ain Borja
(near Super Lait)

ESSAOUIRA

Bazar du Sud Marocain
16 Rue Abdelaziz El Fechtal

Frederic Damgaard
1 Rue Hajjeli

QUEZZANE

Cooperative Artisanale de Tisserands
Quezzane

Pottery

POTTERY IS MADE TODAY THROUGH-out Morocco. Clay kitchen pots, often earth-toned and glazed, are sold outside major towns along the roads. Colorful handmade ceramics are made primarily in Fez and Safi, where centuries-old kilns are still fired up daily. Ready-made ceramics abound, but it is also possible to request special orders for shipping abroad. The majority of Moroccan ceramic styles and colors continue to be the same as those in the 17th and 18th centuries.

FEZ

Fekhari Hamida
Quartier Industriel
Route de Tissa

Custom Craftsmen

LOCALS INEVITABLY HAVE THEIR bedspreads, curtains, furniture, lamps, tiles, doors, and the like crafted by specialized workers in the souk. Unsurpassed craftsmanship is readily available at prices that make Morocco one of the world's least expensive sources for home furnishings. Among the most skillful are the following.

CASABLANCA

Ste. Somatraf
195 Ave. Hassan II
(Plasterwork columns, tables, etc.)

FEZ

Abdou Alaoui
Galerie Helio
15 Rue Karia
(Lamps, lanterns, chandeliers, torchères)

Comatrac
69 Blvd. Mohamed V
(Contemporary wool and cotton fabrics suitable for furniture, curtains, bed-spreads, etc.)

Fekhari Mohamed
Quartier Industriel
Route de Tissa
(Ceramics)

Intexa
150 Blvd. Mohamed V
(Contemporary wool and cotton fabrics suitable for furniture, curtains, bed-spreads, etc.)

Magasin Artisanal
Sabat Lahyadrine, No. 3 V.A.
(Local handicrafts)

MARRAKESH

Boujmiai Ahmed
Souk Essarajine No. 116
(Etched glass)

Kharbibi Moulay Ahmen
Fandak El Amrie Sidi Abdelle
Azize Dar El Bacha No. 10
(Wood carvings)

MIDELT

Soeurs Franciscaines
Kasbah Myriem
(Handmade rugs, linens, bedspreads, etc.)

RABAT

Art Des Oudayas Sur Bois
150 Place des Oudayas
(Wood carvings)

Glossary

agdal—garden

ajjan—mixer of plaster of Paris

bab—monumental gate

bab ed dar—entrance or door

babouches—man's slippers

bejmats—half-bricks enameled on one side and used as floor covering

burnoose—man's hooded cloak, often worn over a *djellaba*

caid—Moslem ruler of a province

chems—small openings in a window, usually made from plaster of Paris with openwork or stained glass

courzya—striped apron worn by Rif Mountain women

dar—house, abode, domain

djellaba—man's robe

fakhkhar—ceramist

fantasia—Berber horseman's display

farrash (pl. *farrasha*)—tile setter who puts *zelliges* directly into a wall

flij—woven strips for tents

gebs (or *jibs*)—plaster of Paris, gypsum, or stucco

ghabbar (pl. *ghabbara*)—artist who joins *zelliges* together, usually with cement and plaster of Paris

haik—woman's dress

hammam—steam bath

hanbel—roughly woven, plain-weave striped blankets and wall hangings made by Berbers

jamur—roof spike made of enameled baked clay or metal with up to five balls of diminishing size and often capped with the national emblem, a star inside a crescent moon

kasbah—desert domain of a single family and dependents

koubbas—tombs of *marabout*, local saints

ksar (pl. *ksour*)—desert tribal fortress sheltering a village community

maallem—master crafter

marabout—local saint

medersa—Moslem institute of higher learning connected to a mosque

medina—the "old town"

mellah—Jewish quarter of a medina

moucharaby—panel of wooden openwork used in balustrades and furniture, also to cover harem windows

pisé—rammed earth

qermud—roof tile

qubba—cupola or dome, often in a main room

rahalia—large decorative plates made in Fez

riyad—inside garden or courtyard

souk—central market, a collection of stalls

sultan—Moslem ruler of the country

tadelakt—Moroccan wall and occasionally floor treatment comparable to Italian stucco, made of sand and quicklime and polished by stone

taksir—cutter of *zelliges*

tizi—mountain pass

vizier—Moslem minister of state

wust ed dar—patio

zawwaq (pl. *zawwaqa*)—craftsman who paints on wood

zelliges—mosaic tiles of enameled terracotta

zwaq—painting on wood

Bibliography

Arthus-Bertrand, Anne and Yann Arthus-Bertrand. *Morocco from the Air*. New York: The Vendome Press, 1994.

Bowles, Paul. *Points in Time*. London: Peter Owen, 1982.

———. *The Spider's House*, New York City: Random House, 1955.

———. *Let It Come Down*. London: John Lehmann, 1952.

———. *The Sheltering Sky*. London: John Lehmann, 1949.

Cox, Madison, et al. *Majorelle: a Moroccan Oasis*. New York: The Vendome Press, London: Thames & Hudson, 1999.

Cross, Mary. *Morocco: Sahara to the Seas*. New York: Abbeville Press, 1999.

D'Ucel, Jeanne. *Berber Art*. Norman, Okla.: University of Oklahoma Press, 1932.

Ellingham, Mark et al. *Morocco: Rough Guide*. London: Rough Guides Limited, 1998.

Flint, Bert. *Tapis et Tissage*. Vol. 2 of *Formes et Symboles dans les Arts Maghrebis*. Tangier: Imprimie E.M.I., 1974.

Fodor's Morocco. New York: Fodor's Travel Publications, Inc., 2000.

Gellner, Ernest. *Muslim Society*. New York: Cambridge University Press, 1983.

Genini, Izza, Jacques Bravo and Xavier Richer. *Splendours of Morocco*. London: I B Tauris & Co. Ltd., 2000.

Hall, Katrina. *The Mosaic Collection: Moroccan*. London: Merehurst Ltd., 2000.

Harris, Walter. *Morocco That Was*. London: Eland Books, 1921.

Hart, David M. *Tribe and Society in Rural Morocco*. London: Frank Cass & Co. Ltd., 2000.

Helou, Anissa and Jeremy Hopley. *Street Café Morocco*. London: Conran Octopus Ltd., 1998.

Hoag, John Douglas. *Western Islamic Architecture*. New York: Braziller, 1963.

Holliday, Jane. *Blue Guide: Morocco* (3rd ed.). New York: W. W. Norton, 1998.

Houatt-Smith, Lisa. *Moroccan Interiors*. Cologne: Benedikt Taschen Verlag, 1995.

Jereb, James F. *Arts & Crafts of Morocco*. London: Thames & Hudson, 1995.

Kapchan, Deborah A. *Gender on the Market: Moroccan Women and the Revoicing of Tradition*. Philadelphia: University of Pennsylvania Press, 1996.

Le Cesne, Delphine, ed. Translated by Tamara Blondel. *Delacroix in Morocco*. Institut du Monde Arabe, 1994.

Maier, John R. and John Maier. *Desert Songs: Western Images of Morocco and Moroccan Images of the West*. New York: State University of New York Press, 1996.

Mayne, Peter. *A Year in Marrakesh*. London: Eland Books, 1982.

Paccard, André. *Traditional Islamic Craft in Moroccan Architecture*. Saint-Jorioz, France: Editions Atelier 74, 1980.

Pandolfo, Stefania. *Impasse of the Angels: Scenes from a Moroccan Space of Memory*. Chicago: University of Chicago Press, 1997.

Phelan, Nancy. *Morocco Is a Lion*. Melbourne: Quartet Books Australia Pty Ltd., 1982.

Pickering, Brooke, Russel Pickering and Ralph Yohe. *Moroccan Carpets*. London: Laurence King, 1998.

Rogerson, Barnaby. *Morocco* (4th ed.). Cadogan Guides, 2000.

Sijelmass, M. *Les Arts Traditionnels au Maroc*. Courbevoie (Paris): ACR Edition/Vilo., 1986.

Smith, Karl. *The Atlas Mountains*. Cicerone Press, 1998.

Textile Museum, Washington, D.C.: *From the Far West: Carpets and Textiles of Morocco*, 1980.

Vogel, Lucien, ed. *Moroccan Silk Designs in Full Color (Dover Pictorial Archive series)*. New York: Dover Publications, Inc., 1996.

Ypma, Herbert. *Morocco Modern*. London: Thames & Hudson, New York: Stewart, Tabori & Chang, 1996.

Acknowledgments

ONE OF THE GREAT PLEASURES IN producing *Morocco* was to meet and work with so many people on both sides of the Atlantic who share our love of this great kingdom. The help, support, and enthusiasm shown to us by the Moroccan National Tourist Office and Moroccan diplomats and government officials, as well as homeowners, hoteliers, designers, and friends living in Morocco, allowed the work on this book to proceed smoothly from its conception.

The prospect of traveling to and from Morocco half a dozen times over the last two years with over three hundred pounds of photography equipment appeared ominous. Mustapha Benkirane, New York general manager of Royal Air Maroc, smoothed the way. Once we had landed, Ambassador Abdeslam Jaidi made sure land arrangements were equally well arranged. Our palace driver, Mohammed Alif, was in constant amazement at the hours we put in, the rough roads we wanted to drive down, the distances we insisted upon covering, and the people, places, and things we photographed. To these gentlemen and all the anonymous people who were always there to help, we say, "Thank you. Without your help, we could not have accomplished so much."

To all the many homeowners who were kind enough to allow us to photograph their properties, we are especially grateful. From Tangier to Taroudant, from Casablanca to Marrakesh, doors to villas, palaces, and apartments were graciously opened to allow us to photograph examples of Moroccan interior design and architecture, much of which had never been recorded before.

It is with tremendous gratitude and with great hope that they will enjoy the fruits of our mutual labors in producing the book that we wish to thank: Issam Lamdouar, director, and Sand Seghrouchni of the Moroccan National Tourist Office, New York City; Ambassador Driss Slaoui; Michel Benisty, Interrent, Casablanca; Jacques Bouriot, director, Mohammed Hammouti, assistant director, and Liliane Boucetta, secretary, as well as the concierge staff, of the Hotel La Mamounia, Marrakesh; Alami Myjat, director general, Hotel Palais Jamai, Fez; Guy Crawford, director general, Hotel Mansour, Casablanca; Bruno Hill, general manager, Hotel Gazelle d'Or, Taroudant;

Jean Paul Lance, former manager of the Hotel Tishka, Marrakesh; Robert Swartzberg, general director, Hotel Minza, Tangier; Louis Bernard, public relations director, Bouygues, Paris.

Very special recognition goes to Bob Ciano, art director, *Travel & Leisure,* and Paige Rense, editor-in-chief, and Tom Sullivan, art director, *Architectural Digest,* who gave us Moroccan assignments. Continued gratitude to photography assistants Andrew Warren, Majid Yadini, and Marc Poujol; photo stylist Claire Lloyd; Dina Davidson, vice president, Duggal Photographic Color Lab, New York City; Connie Uzzo, public relations director, Yves Saint Laurent, Inc., New York City; Christopher Forbes, vice chairman, *Forbes* magazine; Robert Jerofi; Jacqueline Foissac; Bill Willis; T. R. Lawrence and Linda O'Leary, Nomads, Santa Fe, New Mexico; James F. Jereb, The Souk, Santa Fe; Abdou Alaoui; and Missouri Abdelaouhab.

Of special significance was the initial support of the book given by Gael Towey, creative director, *Martha Stewart Living,* when she was at Clarkson Potter. Our gratitude also goes to Roy Finamore. He continued the project and provided skillful picture selection and deft text editing.

Finally, photographers will be interested to know that almost all photographs in the book were shot on Fujichrome Professional 100 film. Bruce Mitchell and Steve Hershel at Fuji headquarters in Carlstadt, New Jersey, and the staff at Polaroid in Cambridge, Massachusetts, were all extraordinarily supportive.

Index